JAMES E. BIRREN

AND

LINDA FELDMAN

Where to Go from Here

DISCOVERING YOUR OWN LIFE'S WISDOM IN THE SECOND HALF OF YOUR LIFE

SIMON & SCHUSTER

SIMON & SCHUSTER
Rockefeller Center
1230 Avenue of the Americas
New York, NY 10020

SIMON & SCHUSTER and colophon are registered trademarks
of Simon & Schuster Inc.

Designed by Karolina Harris

Manufactured in the United States of America

1 2 3 4 5 6 7 8 9 10

Library of Congress Cataloging-in-Publication Data

Birren, James E.
Where to go from here : discovering your own life's wisdom in the second half of
your life / James E. Birren and Linda Feldman.
p. cm.
1. Middle-aged persons—Psychology. 2. Middle age. 3. Self-actualization
(Psychology). 4. Autobiography. I. Feldman, Linda. II. Title.
HQ1059.4.B57 1997
155.6'6—dc21   97-22499
                                                              CIP
ISBN: 978-1-4767-2831-5

To our editor, Mary Ann Naples, who gave life and vision to our project.

—JAMES BIRREN

—LINDA FELDMAN

To the many people who have written their autobiographies, shared their life stories with me, and taught me much about what I know of life. To my children, Barbara, Jeff, and Bruce, and my wife, Betty, who have taught me to listen to life.

—JAMES BIRREN

To my children, Julia and Jason Feldman; my "sisters," Joan Perkell, Patricia Shippee, and Alana Knaster; my friends Riitta and Jonathan Saada; and to Jim Birren, who taught me about life in context.

—LINDA FELDMAN

Philosophy is perfectly right in saying that life must be understood backward. But then one forgets the other clause—that it must be lived forward.

— SØREN KIERKEGAARD,
Journals and Papers, 1843

CONTENTS

PART ONE: PAST: WHERE DID I COME FROM?

Contents

PART TWO:
PRESENT: WHERE
AM I?

PART THREE:
FUTURE: WHERE
AM I GOING?

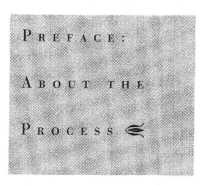

JIM Birren is seventy-eight years old. I'm fifty-five. He's a career scholar and teacher, born in the heartland, who came of age during the Great Depression. I've had five careers; my first home was behind a candy store in Queens, New York, and I grew up in the 1950s dancing to "Earth Angel." Jim's forte is asking the right questions, and I used to have all the answers. He's been married to Betty for fifty-four years. I've been married twice—first time for love and babies, twenty-one years; second time for security, eighteen months. Jim lives a predictable, plotted life. Mine is without a middle ground. He struggles with perfection. For me it's balance.

We met at his well-plaqued office at UCLA—his ego wall, he called it. He never agreed to do an interview with me. He was going to see how the conversation went and then make up his mind. I·was on deadline. After an hour of being looked over, I asked, "Well, will you let me pry into your life?"

In my five years with the *Los Angeles Times* writing the "For Seniors" column, I met outstanding adults. They had lived through terrible times—economic depression, war, death of loved ones, illness—with optimism about the future. Each of my columns was a profile of a person with an indomitable spirit who had found a way, after age sixty, to make the world better.

The story about Jim ran with the headline "You're Never Too Old to Grow Up." I saw in him a serious adult who had a playful side and who was open to people and new ideas. Jim created the practical use of autobiography as a process for people of all ages to look at their lives in context, appreciate all that they've been through, leave the misery behind, and move forward—in other words, to grow up.

After the article, we became friends. I remember driving back to the *Times* office in Santa Monica after one of our weekly lunches thinking that he was really interested in me as a human being. No one had ever asked me the kinds of questions Jim asked. I think that's when our work together really began. I enrolled in the Jim Birren School for Grown-Ups.

Jim doesn't comprehend how he's influenced me. He

didn't direct me to do anything; he simply asked me the right questions, and I asked a few of myself, until I considered the central question of what I was to do with the rest of my life. Somewhere between the time I met him and death I probably would have figured it out without Jim's questions. The inevitables of life do force you to pay attention. But there's something about examining your past that quickens the process and puts you in a more commanding position. I began solving more problems than I created.

When I met Jim I was flirting with being an adult, but I was still in the place where analysis plops its ex-patients: an intellectual limbo not unlike the sensation of wearing cement shoes—I knew where I was at, but I wasn't going anywhere.

I was broke, living with my brother and sister-in-law in a large house overlooking a man-made lake. My room was pretty much the same size as you'd find in a nursing home. But it was there, under the protection of my family, that I flourished. A friend arranged for me to have an office job so that I could still afford to write for the *Times,* and Jim kept asking the tough questions.

Ten months later I owned a new car and a computer, I had saved some money, and I'd signed on with Jim to write this book. I moved into a one-bedroom street-level apartment already occupied by cockroaches. I once timed how long it would take to climb through an already broken window—within three seconds I was securely inside. It had a Beverly Hills address and was across the street from a firehouse. My mother sent me fifty dollars toward buying a steel security door, but I spent it on a massage and slept with a hammer next to my bed.

My desk faced a wall where I had deliberately hung a picture of Georgia O'Keeffe taken by former *Life* magazine photographer Allen Grant. She was sitting inside the doorway of the house she loved in Santa Fe. He had caught a look in her eyes that said, Don't mess with me, I know what I'm doing.

During the first draft of this book, the *Times* downsized and I was miniaturized along with two hundred other journalists and photographers. Part of me felt home free like Br'er Rabbit when he was thrown into the brier patch, and the rest of me felt wounded, unappreciated for work well done.

After filing a farewell column, I went to Oregon to spend time with my son, Jason. I returned to find twenty-three messages on my voice mail and a pile of letters from readers. But it was the phone call from an eighty-two-year-old woman that stayed with me. She said, "What do I have to look forward to tomorrow morning?" Tears streamed down my cheeks, and I realized we were in the same life. Only I had an opportunity to chart a new course and she believed she didn't.

I engineered an ending to my life in Los Angeles by calling everyone in my Rolodex who I knew would wish me well and told each one of them good-bye. I was not afraid life would change. I was afraid of surrendering the very will that had sustained me all my life so that change could occur.

I moved to Santa Cruz—a place I used to call the Bermuda Triangle because students like my daughter, Julia, never left—and rented a little yellow cottage with a lemon tree in the backyard. I hang my laundry out on a line and plant things. I eat tofu. And I learned to appreciate the sunset. Now I applaud with a group of strangers as the last sliver of light disappears beyond the horizon. I'm minutes away from Julia and my granddaughter, Kaya—better known as the brightest star in the universe. The picture of Georgia O'Keeffe still hangs above my computer, only now our eyes have mutuality.

The horror of being an adult is that there is no one to blame for living a life not of your own making. Remember the Laurel and Hardy movie where Stanley asks Ollie what he wants to be reincarnated as? Ollie picks a horse. Stanley says he wants to come back as himself. Ollie ridicules him. In the last scene we see a rather lumpy palomino grazing in an open field and Stanley walking past tipping his hat to the horse. Stanley is back as himself, and he has a long life ahead.

Clearly, the most joyous outcome of the life review process is that you really do treat your past as history, you appreciate your triumphs, and the misery becomes part of the context of your life, not the focus. Like Stanley, you come back as yourself. So I thank Jim Birren for that. It is a gift toward my future, and that's what we hope this book will be for you.

—Linda Feldman

There is no universal map for living a successful second half of life. There is, however, a process that will help chart the course and improve your prospects. For the past twenty years I've acted as a guide for groups of people to tell their life stories. This book can be your guide as you write your autobiography so that you can figure out where to go from here and increase your chances of creating a life that you can call your own. Think of your life as an autobiographical story with a past, a present, and a future yet to be plotted.

Any age is a good age to take an inventory of one's life. I think midlife, where a rich store of experience is available for piecing together, is the best time to pause, review, and eventually approach your long future with assurance and optimism. It's also time to appreciate yourself and understand the uniqueness of your particular predicament in life.

This is not a how-to book with some magic-carpet ride to a blissful future of happy elderhood. There is magic out there, but it is going to take an experienced mind to sort it out. The late scientist Jonas Salk described his work to Bill Moyers as finding the logic in the magic. My sense is that ours is no less a task, though you probably think there isn't anything magical about your life. My guess is that Salk didn't know what he was going to find, either, until he used a microscope.

Sometimes you have to take a walk around a temple in Thailand. A close friend visited Thailand recently. She is a graduate of every self-help seminar and guru-led weekend retreat for self-actualization known to a Californian. But it took a mile walk around the wall of an ancient temple to give her the most important insight of all.

On the ground along the length of the temple wall, from corner to corner, were hundreds of brass bowls. The custom is to drop a coin into each bowl as you walk past it, and as the coin clinks into the bowl you recite something you are blessed with.

She dropped her coin in bowl one and said, "I am blessed with good health." In bowl two it was good friends, and then her lovely house, Mozart, being a size six, and dolphins. When she looked ahead at all of the remaining bowls she felt this enormous ache of sadness because she thought she had nothing else to say.

Yet she finished the walk, not missing a bowl, thankful for the smile of a taxi driver, the look on a friend's face when she surprised her with a gift, the color of her favorite rose.

She continues the ritual in her own home with some bowls she brought back with her.

The point is that she didn't necessarily come away enlightened, as she had thought she did from all her spiritual capers only to relapse into the doldrums. She took pause. She acknowledged the little kindnesses, the incidentals of life. And most importantly, she discovered new meanings. Blessings are everywhere. We have to learn to appreciate them and note them. The magic comes when you begin to see things differently.

Over the years, whenever I asked older students what, if any, regrets they had, one theme emerged: looking back, they wished they had taken more chances to be themselves. They thought their greatest obstacle was their own nature and the limitations they themselves created. An examined life unlocks enough emotional armor so that an uncommon freedom of expression and intellect can flourish, and so that you can get out of your own way.

Your life story has a power all its own. Once you document your life and realize all that you have been through, survived, and accomplished, you can't help but have a fresh view of your worth. When you're armed with a sense of worth, you're armed with the power of self-respect. If your life feels empty and meaningless, there's also power in knowing what's missing.

There are different ways of telling your life story. I like to walk and talk rather than sit in a chair and ruminate. My wife, Betty, likes to fold up her legs on a couch and talk. Maybe I'm a little hyperactive and need to relax when I talk to others or about myself. When I'm outdoors, I permit the distraction of a dog or a beautiful rose while I think about my own answers.

Every Saturday morning at eight-thirty sharp, three to six folks meet at my house, and we all start off for a rigorous four-hour walk in the Santa Monica Mountains. It's amazing to me how many interesting and stored-away parts of our life stories we get into as we walk along. Skeletons can be exhumed, more often with laughs than with dread. Digging them up helps us get over the next hill or into the next week, and once they're dug up, there's no need to dig in that hole again.

I remember one walk where we were all competing to tell the worst things that had happened to us recently. The idea came to me to create the MAGS—the Moan and Groan Society. Each week we gave an award to the person with the most interesting moan and groan.

The idea caught on and we spent some weeks with it, then moved on to still another idea: the GOYAS—the Get

Off Your Ass Society—recognized the person who had ini-
tiated something new during the week.

Eventually we all have to get going, but we are better
prepared by knowing the intention behind the action.
There's a Hebrew-based word, "kavvanah," which is the
spirit behind the intention that lifts everyday acts to higher
realms. It literally means "take aim."

It's important to air yourself out, and for me, taking a
walk in the mountains with a group of jovial people loos-
ens my mind and tongue and provides material for later
writing.

Organizing your life story is like describing your walk
through life. This includes the potholes, what the good guys
and bad guys did to you, and how chance played its role.

Gore Vidal titled his memoir *Palimpsest,* which literally
means a type of paper prepared for writing on and wiping
out again. He likened his memoir writing to "discrete ar-
cheological layers of a life to be excavated like the different
levels of old Troy, where, at some point beneath those
cities upon cities, one hopes to find Achilles and his beloved Patroclus, and all that wrath with which our world
began."

I'd like to take you all along on Saturday mornings and
chat with you about where you can go from here. Instead,
I offer you this book to help you excavate the layers of
your Troy.

What you truly own in life are your memories and the imagination to create new ones. Are you ready to add them up and see where they lead you?

Am I Ready for a Review?

Any time you're thinking about the future is a good time to look back at your past. Some people are not sure they are ready to tell their life stories. Most often that's because they think there isn't much to tell or because they fear telling secrets. Let me assure you that out of the most ordinary lives come some great stories, and I ought to know after listening to them for twenty years.

You remember your own life by documenting what mattered most to you. And if you just do that, you will discover the connections between then and now and the wisdom of how you managed to come this far.

"After all," Gore Vidal wrote in *Palimpsest,* "one's recollected life is just about all that's left at the end of the day when the work is done and gone, property now of others."

My sense is that writing a life story signals that you might have to dig up an old garden or two, and that feels like confessing secrets. My rule is this: If what's under a rock isn't important to you, there's no need to dig it up. We're interested in your life story, not a confession of all your sins. Remember, what you reveal is as interesting as what you leave out.

After all these years of experience with autobiography groups, I've found that men tend to be slower to realize the value of telling their story, and I suspect that's because of the notion that men are doers, not talkers.

A retired policeman told me he tried twice to join an autobiography group, but both times he backed off at the last moment. I knew that he had an interesting career, and though he was shy about telling details about his personal life, I was convinced the group would have brought him around.

When he backed out for the second time, he told me, "I guess I'm not ready for it yet." He couldn't articulate what "it" meant. The unknown can be intimidating.

One of the benefits of looking at your life as a personal history lesson is that you might dig up insights and leave rusty relics behind, raising the possibility that you will have to change. As interested as people are in change, they are also hesitant to let go of old habits, even if they are too rusty for modern use. If you're interested in knowing where to go from here, you have to know where you've been.

A Greek man I invited to join an autobiography group told me that Greek men don't do that sort of thing. But he surprised me and joined the group anyway, and he talked about being a boy in Greece during World War II when the Germans were in control of his country.

He told us how he risked being shot when he jumped into a moving German supply truck and threw food to his family. I think he told these war stories of his boyhood for the first time. We still send each other Christmas cards.

I can remember the conflict that Sister Margaret, a Catholic nun, had about her commitment to serve God and telling her story to a group that might have non-Catholics or non-believers in it. She felt that one should talk to God about one's life, not to strangers. She felt that her life story might not be appreciated by others, but the surprise for her was that the less religious listeners were unusually moved by her stories of life in a religious community and by the depth of her commitment.

Sister Margaret's fear is at the heart of all the reluctance —the fear that your life might not be appreciated. Once you begin to understand your own life, that fear will disappear.

CHAPTER 1

You're Never Too Old to Grow Up ≤

PEOPLE usually ask me two questions about writing their life stories. The first one—Why should they do it?—is the easy one. You should do it because it's a big step forward in developing a sense of direction in your life while taking with you the best of your past. Putting together a picture of your life not only helps you to understand it better but helps you to accept yourself more after seeing what you've been through. You gain the strength to plot your own future after you understand your past.

The second question—When should I write it?—is a tough one. There's no single answer, but my sense is that you should write your story when you admit that the future doesn't look clear, when you feel as if there's something missing, when the social rules and popular behavior that have governed your life for so long no longer feel appropriate.

You may wake up one morning and feel as if you're going through the motions of a former life. The thrill is gone, as the song goes. Some people feel a sense of loss, perhaps misperceived as a loss of purpose or youth. But most of us experience something like neutral gear. The motor is still running, but you're not going anywhere.

If you're not used to standing still, you might fear you're in a rut. This is the void in which you discover the self-help seminars, retreats, and how-to books. Or you might revisit the religion of your childhood or trade it in for a different one. Physically, you have less vitality. Emotionally, you may feel ambivalent. Intellectually, if you are well endowed, you are probably dumbfounded that someone as smart as you could be so unproductive. The rest of us may realize that this might be as far as we can go. Spiritually, we feel a great need to find something more important than ourselves to believe in.

I think this is the time to assess where you've come from so that you'll know where you are and where you're going. I think this is when you begin to sense that your life has a limited duration. How we use whatever time is left will define who we are.

We need to look back in order to move forward. Most people are struggling to live a life they want to be in, a life that has balance and financial security as well as more personal decision-making. Sometimes we need to take stock in order to improve our lot.

Robert Butler, M.D., who coined the phrase "life review," said that the "elemental" things of life—children, friendship, nature, sensual awareness—assume greater significance as people sort out the more important from the less important.

We all need some sense of the future, too. What's so terrifying about people living in the streets, especially the ones who choose to, is that they have absolutely no sense of the future. It seems they have missed or lost all the opportunities to fulfill their potential as well as the desire to create new ones.

I'm reminded of an article I read recently about the pianist Menahem Pressler who made his Carnegie Hall debut solo recital at age seventy-two. His recital, he said, "should be an example to my students that one should never give up or miss an opportunity that life presents to you." He went on to say, "Here I have a situation where fate, which has often been so good to me, offered a challenge that I simply could not dismiss." But it was what he said about practicing the piano that really struck me. He said it was in the practice that the search for music takes place, where the deep moments are felt. The performance may represent only a part of his capacity.

And so it is with this journey we will take together. Clarity brings focus. Attaining this clarity is part of the journey. What you do with it once you have it is important, but it's in the journey where all the deep moments are experienced.

The journey you are about to embark on will be traveled over familiar territory, and yet there is no simple map. Examining your life takes guts and humor. But I know of no better way to enjoy your own company or honor yourself, especially if you decide to write it all down as an autobiography. And if you're fortunate enough to be part of a group, you'll appreciate the strengths of other people. The group itself will become one of the vehicles in your journey.

The Sufi poet Rumi tells us to think of our lives as if we had been sent by a king to a distant country with a special task. The blessed few, like Mozart and Shakespeare, knew their calling early on in life. They were blessed, but their challenge was no easier than ours. They had to improve themselves continually.

All of us mortals are on a journey to make a life for ourselves that is meaningful. "You might do a hundred other things," says the poet, "but if you fail to do the one thing for which you were sent it will be as if you had done nothing."

I think we are all searching for the meaning that Rumi suggests and the contentment that comes with its fulfillment. But, a Mozart aside, I also think that what was meaningful when you were seventeen may turn out to seem very different when you're twenty-seven or forty-seven.

Branching Trees and Other Metaphors

There are certain points in your life where you could have gone in any number of directions, yet one path was chosen, either by you or your parents or circumstances. I call these moments branching points.

If you think of your life as a branching tree, then at what point do the various branches grow? These are the turning points in your life. Where did they take you?

When I lead the members of one of my autobiography groups through the writing of their life stories, one of the first things I do is pass out sheets of graph paper for use as props to get the memory going. Starting with your birth story, you rank the highs and lows of your life with dots. Then you draw your lifeline.

My birth, for instance, was a real minus because, in the confusion of the delivery room, I fell on the floor by accident. Not an auspicious beginning, but one that shaped my life.

Imagine a graph of your life. Think about your branching points. How do you remember them? Plus or minus? How important was each point to your life as a whole? If you could represent a branching point as a dot, where would you place it on your imaginary lifeline?

I have charted my lifeline, the ups and downs, starting with a dot at minus thirty-five for my birth, as you can see in the graph that follows. When you set out to create your own graph, you will place your birth dot, graph the main highs and lows of your life, and then draw lines to connect the dots. Most people have more highs than lows, but surprisingly, before they actually put those dots on the page, they didn't see it that way. Think of the graph as a canvas for a life painting, and all the points on it make up the bigger picture.

Looking at my lifeline, I see many high points during my twenties. That's when I went to graduate school, met my wife, Betty, and got married. But I rate the birth of my children as somewhat lower than my marriage because they were born during a time when I was busy working and not making enough money. Now I view with joy their birth as high points.

Although life must be lived by moving forward, it is best understood by comprehending what we've lived through. If we look back, think of how we felt about an event of the past, and then reflect on how we feel about that same event now, the event usually doesn't seem as bad as we thought it was years ago.

Here are some questions to help you plot your lifeline:

What events do the dots on your lifeline represent?

Who else was involved?

What relationship did that person have to you?

How did each event influence your life?

How did you feel at the time?

What was the lesson?

Why did your life grow one way and not another?

Were you responsible for these events, or were they bigger than you and imposed on you from the outside?

Which events made a difference in your life? (The ones that made a difference become your branching points.)

My father didn't earn much money after World War I, so he moved us from Chicago to a rural area. He came by train to see us on weekends. My mother never locked the door or worried about me. I used to go off and visit the farmers in the area. I remember one day riding down our street holding the reins of a horse-drawn wagon sitting next to a farmer I had met that morning.

Looking back, I see that period of my life as a serious branching point because it gave me an intrinsic optimism about life. I was this little kid from a big city transplanted to a rural area with gravel streets and cows roaming about.

The feeling of expansiveness in my life came from this branching point. Of course, I wouldn't have known it at the time. You don't think about those things when you're

My Lifeline

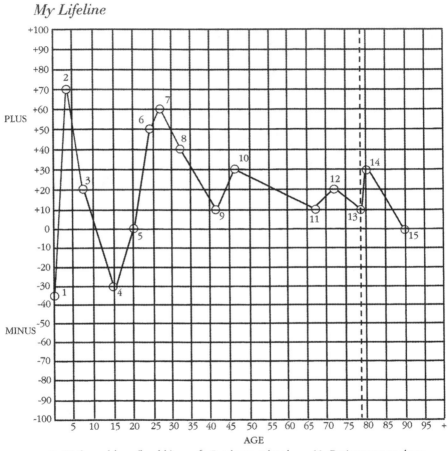

1. Birth problem (health)
2. Moving to a rural area
3. Starting school
4. Struggle with religion
5. Finishing junior college
6. Graduate school
7. Marriage
8. Family
9. Career contraction
10. Career expansion
11. Retirement as dean
12. New university position
13. Retirement
14. Completion of books
15. Death

Your Lifeline

Put a dot at your age for each major event or branching point in your life. Rate the event according to how good or bad you feel about it, somewhere between plus to minus 100 percent. Draw a vertical dotted line at your present age. Put a dot at the age you expect to live to, and rate how you expect to feel about the next years. Connect all the dots to complete your lifeline chart.

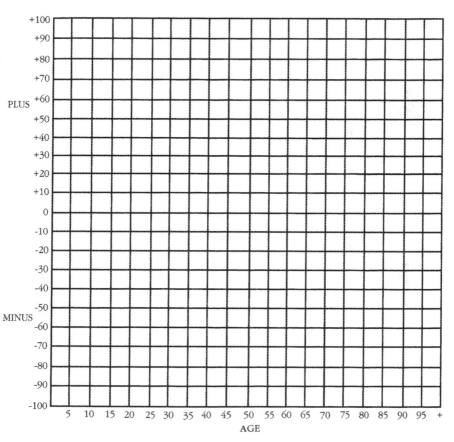

five. But now, at my age, if I ask myself the question "Why am I an organic optimist?" I can say with assurance that it goes back to that period.

My father's inability to make a lot of money wasn't a catastrophe. In fact, it was probably one of the best things that ever happened to me. To this day I expect change to be positive; I'm not afraid of it.

So look first at your strengths in respect to a branching point. You might recall that you went through hell at the time, maybe even considered suicide, but looking back, and in the context of other branching points, you're certainly glad today you didn't take any drastic action. Try to see your life story more as personal history and less as a psychological drama.

Be careful here not to fall into the "what if?" trap. Our journey in this book is to move into the future by learning from the past, not by bemoaning it. If you try to rewrite your life based on what you know now, eventually the "what ifs" will become an obstacle to moving forward.

The early branching points of our lives are usually a result of someone else's decision or of the times in which we live. For instance, most women of my generation did not have careers. Their personal ambition was pretty much overruled by the demands of family life and societal attitudes against women working outside of the home. Women were rarely appreciated for their intellect alone.

Imagine how Willa Cather was received when she wrote in her 1915 novel, *The Song of the Lark,* "Who marries who is a small matter, after all." Women in literature, even if they were courageous or rigorous thinkers, were understood only in terms of marriage, adultery, and love. Even Joan of Arc, brave as she was, was characterized as delusional.

If you're a woman my age and you decide to write your life story, you will want to consider the times in which you grew up rather than mourn a lost career that did not gain acceptance until twenty or more years later. The same is true if you were a child of a Depression-era family. You probably had no control over what happened to you during those times. I remember hearing wrenching stories of how families escaped the Oklahoma dust storms and arrived in California in broken-down automobiles, poor and destitute.

It is important to understand *how* your life flowed the way it did as opposed to analyzing your life. You may have been devastated by the family house burning down, but when you moved to a new town, perhaps you met someone who influenced your life profoundly.

Even now in your adult years your background still influences your decisions. I'm reminded of the woman who came to California to pursue a career but who returned home to the East to take care of her aging parents. Returning home was a major branching point for her but the sense of responsibility she used to make her decision counts for something. She can either understand this branching point as something to regret or as a demonstration of her value system and a source of self-esteem.

> *What are the lifelong threads that hold the fabric of your life together?*

Instead of resembling a branching tree, maybe your life has been more like a tapestry with a few strong threads holding it all together. Most of us have five or six important threads running through our lives. These continuous threads—family, career, money, optimism, religion—are woven into all the important events.

One middle-aged woman told me her life wasn't like a tapestry *or* a branching tree. It was more like crabgrass. She anchored in one place for a while, put down roots, and then sent out a runner for the next place to root. She told me that she was a gypsy by nature and until she felt homesick she'd probably continue to live this way.

I remember a Japanese professor who, as a child in Japan, was placed in a camp during World War II. The authorities assured parents that their children would be safer outside of the major cities. He told me he came to recognize that the reason children were placed in this camp was to act as a deterrent to the American amphibious forces that were expected to land close by. What would the Americans do when faced with so many children? His perception was not that he was put into a protected place but that he was used as part of a defense strategy. He saw himself as a pawn. That was a major branching point for him, and he chose to describe his life as a branching river. The camp experience and a later bout with tuberculosis limited his life, and the river narrowed. When his life expanded, the river broadened.

The Japanese professor's flowing-river image suited him better than the branching-tree metaphor did because sometimes, as when he became ill, his life had no direction at all, and at other times he felt as if his life flowed backward. He also saw his life broadening and deepening at times, and that didn't fit

> *Has your life developed like a branching tree, a winding river, or crabgrass? Or is it a huge unfolding tapestry with a few major threads?*

with the branching-tree image. When I saw the picture he drew of a bending river with the twists and turns numbered so they would prompt his memory when he wrote his life story, I agreed with him that it was a good picture of how he saw his life.

Many of you will see your lives as a combination of all these things. Whatever metaphor you use, the objective is to prime your memory. Just as you can't look straight into the sun, you can't stare straight into your soul for answers. So a little sensitizing helps to get the memories flowing.

Memory Primers: Animals and Shields

When I was growing up in the country we used old iron hand pumps to pump water from wells. Sometimes the pump would just squeak its dry cry when we pushed the handle up and down. The only way to get it going again was to prime it by pouring some water down through the top.

In a way, that's what we're doing now—priming your memory supply. Once it starts to flow, you'll be amazed at yourself.

Native Americans used animal metaphors to connect a person to the mystery of life and to teach humans lessons. For our purposes, imagining yourself as an animal will act as a memory primer and maybe expose something about you that might not otherwise surface.

> *What kind of an animal would you like to be? What kind of an animal are you really like? How would your friends answer that question about you?*

I remember someone answering, "I'm really a workhorse, I go out every day and work hard and bring home money, but I would like to be an eagle. I think my friends would say I'm a hen, someone who looks after others."

Those are wonderful contrasting images. He was saying, "I'm a responsible person, but I would really like to be an eagle and soar." He felt a great hunger for freedom, grace, and beauty and the ability to fly over life. He perceived public opinion of him in the passive form of a hen.

One woman wanted to be a tigress, but she saw herself as a cat. She said her best friend thought she was a kitten. Although the cat personality, with its aloofness and independence, runs through her, there's an interesting contrast between the domestic and the primitive, the fierce and the playful.

I want to be a dolphin because they're free and smart. But I'm really more like a stag. I try to dominate a herd, taking on obligations and responsibilities.

Another memory primer I use is similar to a Native American ritual of personal shield-making. During marriage ceremonies the shields of the bride and the groom revealed the inner secrets of one partner's soul to the other. Shields were also used to depict their owners' talents and usefulness to the tribe.

Women usually made their own shields, but men did not. A brother was chosen to make the man's shield, preventing the bridegroom's male ego from getting in the way of truth.

Presenting yourself untruthfully on a shield was a disgrace, and those shields were burned in a mourning ceremony. Can you imagine the heat from the shields of today's candidates for public office?

Our shields are invisible, but we all have strengths and weaknesses, gifts, and purposes. What would you put on your shield? One man I remember wrote two words—"oldest son"—to describe himself. The other men in the group reacted with surprise, especially when he said he had to go home to Korea to take care of his parents and the family book, which listed all of his relatives going back twenty-five generations. For him there was no reason to list his other characteristics: every one of them was contingent on his position as the oldest son.

All of the experiences of your life have brought you to this moment in time, for better or for worse. Nowhere can you find better clues to yourself than by trying to integrate the life you have already lived.

Let me once again quote the late Dr. Jonas Salk on this point because he describes so eloquently how he approached his work: Finding the logic in the magic. What his words mean to me is that all the answers are within our grasp; we just have to be astute enough to recognize them in the creative chaos of our lives. We also need to examine them from a wide perspective while trusting our feelings and being faithful to our personal truths.

Mobilizing enough spirit to want to look at your life is worth the effort because, if nothing else, you emerge with a clear picture of how well you have adapted. Your triumphs more than make up for the low points.

I know a man who served in the army during the Vietnam War. He was a graduate of a theological school, spoke Spanish, and could type. He was put in charge of writing up officers' physical examinations. He was ordered to make up acceptable blood pressure ratings and other exam results, and if he didn't do so, he would be put on kitchen duty.

When he was discharged, what he had done stuck with him. He earned a Ph.D. and is now a professor of ethics in a prominent western university where he has become an expert on the ethics of death and dying.

Once you blow the dust off your experiences, even your shortcomings are better balanced and the tensions they once caused will subside or, as in the case of the Vietnam veteran, will shape your future. My friend who falsified medical records knew he couldn't make up for what he had done, nor could he just live his life as if it hadn't happened. He used the tension of the army branching point to shape his life in a positive way. And with no excuses. He is neither a victim of the corruption of the army nor a victim of his own lack of integrity. What could have been a breaking point for him was instead a powerful branching point.

The branching tree, or whatever metaphor you choose, along with the animal images and the creation of your personal shield all help to provoke memories about you and your life. Good questions, like an astronaut's debriefing, seek to fill in the rest of the picture and get you started on the telling of your life story.

Just as an astronaut, after traveling through space, comes back to earth to be debriefed by his colleagues about his voyage, we all need the assistance of some appropriate questions to make sense out of our lives. Think of this process as a form of debriefing.

I know people who go back to the house they grew up in, sit in the room where they once slept, and allow the memories to wash over them. Allow yourself a journey back into your life. Even the potholes have meaning.

PART ONE

Past: Where Did I Come From?

CHAPTER 2

What Kind of a Hand Was I Dealt? ✍

Y O U are what you remember.

Memories, a combination of personal mythology and reconstructed history, define the life you've lived to this moment in time. All the information you need to know to make the connections between then and now is within the confines of your own memory. Your life story, filled with paradoxes and contradictions, riddled with ambivalence and fears, and every so often honored by triumph, is as unique as a fingerprint.

Just as fingerprints identify certain qualities unique about you, telling your life story reveals the person who did all the living—your *self*. I believe it is within our grasp to truly *be* ourselves, comfortable in our own skin. Unfortunately, many of us haven't yet found that comfort. I think that's because we're searching outside of ourselves as if there were one answer, one self, and one journey toward the acquisition of wisdom.

By telling your life story you reveal your own life's wisdom, and that's why autobiography has such an impact on people. Once you sort through what author Joyce Carol Oates calls "the inventory of our lives," you can't help but be impressed by how you've managed to come this far. The question is, where do you go from here?

If you're a bit snarled in the present, the natural course is to return to the beginning of your life. The irony is that so many of your essential ideas about life developed during a time when you had little control over events. I'd like to help you look in the right places for important pieces of your history so that you can tell your life story in a way that will have meaning for you.

Think of me as a guide you've asked along on a fishing expedition. You could have the best equipment and the right bait, but if you don't know where the fish are, you're going to come back empty-handed.

Part one of autobiography is history gathering—more about the "what was" without the "why it was." Asking "why" questions can be distracting. Any schoolchild, when asked a "why" question, will probably give an "I don't know" answer, because "why" implies "you shouldn't have."

Test it on yourself: Why did you study piano? What was

it about the piano that made you want to play? My guess is that the "what" question elicits more insights than the truth-seeking "why" question. Memories are not necessarily about truth. They are a record of your perceptions, from which you have constructed what you call the truth about yourself.

If you think of your life story as a fingerprint, you'll have an easier time figuring out what was authentic about your life and what was a facsimile prescribed by a combination of Madison Avenue, your peers, Hollywood, your parents, and other pressures. What is indelible and how much can be erased without your ever noticing it's gone?

Sometimes I use the metaphor of a poker game to explain how much of your early history was simply a given —the hand you were dealt—and still more of your history was spent on playing out that hand using imperfect knowledge and having little control of the results.

Let's say as soon as you're born you're in this imaginary card game. Picture yourself clad in a diaper, unable to lift your head up without support, unable to eat by yourself, get around, or speak your undeveloped mind. No matter. The game begins anyway.

In our card game, there are four original suits representing what is given to you at birth as well as two wild cards. You could do nothing to change that important first hand of family, home, money, and health. You were born with a certain set of traits into a family that provided a home funded by monies accrued by people who were responsible for your well-being. Yet all of these memories are part of the history that still influences you.

The wild cards I just mentioned are more complicated. I call one of them your nature, though sometimes people use terms like "spirit" or "temperament." Your nature joins you to the human family and isolates you from it at the same time.

I once asked a philosopher friend how much destiny influenced our lives. He said that the human could be described like a missile guidance system, programmed by certain variables to go in a certain direction. But he added that a slight alteration can change the destination. And that's where I think your own nature intervenes. I believe that we can intervene on our own behalf and alter the course of our lives by plotting a new path.

But any plotting must acknowledge the other wild card —life itself. For as long as you stay in the game, life's surprises and catastrophes intrude into every move you make. Surprise and catastrophe immobilize us or force us to move forward. No one has found the formula to avoid pain, but there are many ways to express how we suffer it. I'm always reminded of Hemingway's observation: "The world breaks everyone and afterward many are strong at the broken places." The point is not to question "why pain?" or "why me?" but to learn from ourselves and others how the pain was endured.

The start of the story is birth. The occasion of your birth changed some people's lives, although there probably wasn't a bright star in the sky heralding the blessed event. The circumstances of the day you were born also made a certain imprint on your life. It is the story of how we began our lives and who was important and how it all happened.

In Chapter 1, I suggested that you give your birth story a grade. I gave mine a minus thirty-five because minutes after I was born I fell on the floor of the delivery room. The attending physician and the nurse both left the room to get an umbilical clip and left me on a table adjacent to my mother. Apparently during their absence she expelled the placenta and the weight of it pulled me down onto the floor.

Many years later she told me that she would never forget the look on the doctor's face when he came back into the room and saw her baby—a purple mess on the floor. She also told me that my father shot dice the night before in order to win the money to pay the hospital bill.

When my mother left the hospital with me, the nursery attendant told her I was better now. Better than what? My sense is that neither the hospital staff nor my mother thought I would survive, which explains why I never received a birth certificate. Twenty years later I had to fill out a form, which made me one of the few "babies" whose record of birth is in their own handwriting.

And so I arrived at the poker table of life with no official record of my birth and a foggy prognosis as to whether or not I would ever hold my own cards.

What's your birth story? How has it made its impression on you as you look back on the details? Are there family stories about it? What do you know of your earliest history? How did you arrive at the poker table?

When I asked Linda to write her birth story it was something that didn't seem to be any big deal for her. She had heard the story told and retold over the years and had never attached any great significance to it. But to humor me, she did call her mother and ask her to retell it for the record.

Although Linda's parents lived in Queens, New York, the family doctor had offices in Brooklyn. Since the family did not own a car, Linda's mother traveled by subway to Brooklyn each month for regular examinations. When it became clear that baby Linda was coming, her father called a taxi to take them on the thirty-minute trip. The new parkway, the most direct route, was not yet open, so when the taxi appeared at the entrance, the workmen stopped it from going any farther. Linda's mother yelled from the backseat that the baby was coming and demanded that the road be unofficially opened immediately. No one argued with a woman about to have a baby. A police escort was quickly organized to lead the way.

And so, in a blaze of sirens, they arrived at the hospital. Thirty hours later, despite earlier calculations, Linda made her official entrance into the world with a typical wail. Her mother, hearing her cry, yelled back: "What's she screaming about? I'm the one who suffered the pain."

The mother-daughter conflict was born in that first encounter, but it wasn't until Linda actually wrote it down that she saw its genesis. She had sat down at the poker table with a formidable adversary—her mother. Although she arrived heralded by sirens signaling a big to-do, the lifelong hostility in the hand she was dealt overshadowed many other events and influenced her judgment. Throughout her life she would spend a lot of time trying to win her mother over. And a lot of time fighting her off.

Linda's emotional health card was affected by the drama of her birth, but some of the health cards we are dealt leave lifelong physical effects. One of my group members, Peter, had a heart murmur when he was little, and his parents were warned to treat everything about his health seriously. When he had a sniffle, he was sent right to bed to get over it. He grew up a fragile child.

Not until he was required to submit to a college entrance physical examination did he find out that the heart murmur had disappeared. But his self-image as a sickly child was so profoundly embedded that he continued to protect himself from overexertion.

During Peter's senior year, many of his classmates traveled abroad, but even though he was physically fit, he turned down the opportunity. He remembered questioning himself and felt caught between his fear of becoming an invalid and his eagerness to see the world. Instead of traveling, he took up the study of geography. Finally, in his fifties, armed with the simple fact that he had lived for five healthy decades, he became an explorer and traveled the world. He remembered the day he applied for his passport: "I was freed from my past, which had held hostage a sickly child who was going to take it easy for the rest of his life."

Another group member, Jerry, became deaf when a common ear infection was treated with a high-risk antibiotic. Despite losing his hearing Jerry had the kind of nature that changed how things might have turned out. Instead of becoming reclusive, he became an athlete and a scholar.

When he played baseball, he watched the ball and the hand signals of coaches. All of his time off the field was spent reading. "Deafness didn't hold me back," he told the group. "I read more, and that put me ahead in school. I graduated number one in my high school class."

All of us are dealt genetic cards at birth: hair and eye color, being short or tall, and much of the way we look. There's a lot of tension about these traits in all of our early histories. We all have certain limitations, but part of the process of grow- ing up is accepting those real or imagined constraints and resolving the tensions they create. The most interesting life stories are about ordinary people who overcome the wild card obstacles of life and the dark forces of their own natures.

> *What kind of health cards were you dealt at birth and along the way? How did you choose to experience pain?*

Family

Our earliest experiences with pain and pleasure occur within our family. Try to recall what you knew about your mother and father and what their relationship was like with each other and with you.

I have always been fascinated with how little information we have about our parents even though we've spent so many years in their presence. Do you know what kind of lives they dreamed about for themselves? Who were their most powerful influences? Where did they get some of their important ideas?

Most of us wouldn't know the answers to these questions

unless our parents wrote an autobiography. As children we interpreted the world through a simple screening device. If our basic needs were satisfied, we considered the world friendly. If we were deprived, the world seemed hostile. Parents either did or did not satisfy our needs. Our earliest parental database was contained in one file labeled "provider." Throughout our childhood all that we knew about our parents' lives could be found in that file. As we got older we added material, but the general category could be found under the title "me." We rarely separated our parents as individuals from their role as parents until we became adults, and then we suddenly wanted them to be our cheering squad.

Although my parents had only an elementary school education, they encouraged me to go as far as I wanted. Looking back, I'd say they were loving, supportive, and simple in their orientation to life. Even when I received some recognition for research I had done, I had the impression that my mother was saying to me, "Jim, that's nice, but are you getting enough sleep and good food to eat?" I wanted her to praise me as a scientist, not worry about my food groups.

I recall a story about a famous Hollywood director who finished shooting his first movie. He asked the studio to arrange for a screening room so that he could show his immigrant parents what he had accomplished. They took their first airplane trip across the country and sat for two hours with their son watching his movie, just the three of them. When it was over, the father asked, "What happened to the newsreel?" Instead of praising his son's achievement, the father asked about what was missing. The father was back in the 1940s when newsreels were part of every movie bill. The son was showing off his first film in the modern screening room of a major film studio.

These parents didn't have much to offer, but they didn't hold their son back. The director laughs now when he tells that story. After all, he did make the movie, it did win an Academy Award, and whatever the problem was with his parents, it certainly wasn't catastrophic. But at the time he thought his parents didn't care about his work.

Humor moves people from seeing life as a series of problems to looking at it with greater insight and mastery. At a certain point in our lives, we do want to move from coping to mastery over the events of the past.

Science fiction author Ray Bradbury detoured around his parents and experienced them differently. "I followed my own passions and imagination," he said. "My parents knew I was nuts but never said so. I felt loved because they left me alone, and so I always believed in myself."

On the other hand, many children of famous parents—

no matter if their father saved the world from tyranny or their mother developed a lifesaving vaccine—bemoan the fact that they were neglected by a selfish parent.

The family card is not designed with the next generation in mind. It is a product of the times and the personalities of those who are in charge of the deal.

Linda's first-generation American family numbered twenty-one when they all sat down together for a holiday meal, the kids at one table and the grown-ups at another. Many of them lived close enough together so that running away from home meant going to an aunt's house for sanctuary. Linda could always get love somewhere. In her early childhood years, relatives moved in and out of her house, and every room had a dual purpose. During the day there was a dining room, but at night it was Aunt Fran's bedroom. One permanent resident was her European-born grandmother. She couldn't read or write in any language, but she signed her *X* and permitted her sixteen-year-old son, Al, to serve in World War II.

For most teenagers, one of the signs of being an adult was getting a car. For Linda, it was being allowed to join in the family poker game. Poker was not simply a metaphor for life, it was a part of her life. In her family, the poker game was a family ritual which, for new inductees, meant learning the rules and winning or losing with the grown-ups. No one made concessions for her.

Looking back, she told me that was how she learned to be a good sport, not only about losing but about winning as well. Her father reinforced what she learned at the poker table with the game of baseball. "Give it your all," he used to tell her, "and you'll never have anything to be ashamed of."

I remember the sense of relief a group member named Marcus had when he wrote, "I came from a dishonest family. Even my father's brother cheated him." Marcus was acutely aware of the character of his family through his father's experience. As a child, he would overhear his father and uncle arguing. He grew up disliking the man who cheated his father, and he was ashamed of his family. He remembered never being allowed to see his cousins until he was an adult. Marcus came from a disreputable family, but the turmoil was out in the open. He grew up suspicious but committed to being an honest person himself.

Louise described her family as so awful that she remembered from the time she was in elementary school wanting to leave home. Her stepfather drank a great deal, and her house smelled of alcohol. "I came to think of myself as a survivor," she told me, "and that broke my connection with my family. Even when I was a young child, I used to think I wasn't going to be beaten down. I was tough and in charge of my life."

Louise married when she was still a teenager so that she

could move out of her house. The marriage was a disaster, but she survived, became tougher, and left that house, too. "I spent my childhood protecting myself and my early adult years surviving until I realized that, yes, I was a survivor but I was alone," she said. Louise joined a church and for the first time in her life felt accepted. She helped others and, through her work for others, became a part of a "family."

Alcohol appears in many life stories. Allen watched his father drink away his job and his health. He vowed never to be like him. "But I slipped into drinking when I married a mentally sick woman and had two children to worry about," he said. "I drank myself all the way to the bottom and thought I would die."

Allen joined Alcoholics Anonymous, sobered up, and, like Louise, helped others to stop drinking. He realized he liked helping people and allowing them to help him. When he wrote his life story he saw how close he had come to living his father's story. "I realized I didn't have to be like my immigrant father, who tried to drink away uncertainty. I could be dry and change what was creating my misery."

Not all life stories have the theme of surviving and overcoming an unfortunate family life. Sometimes people have family models that are almost too positive. Roy said that he used to feel embarrassed because he couldn't think of anything bad to say about his family. Still, he was adrift for most of his early adult years and couldn't figure out what to do with himself. He tried different jobs but nothing gave him satisfaction. When he thought about his family, he said, "Everyone in my family seemed to be a success and a good person. I thought I could never be like any of them, so I took jobs that they would never have accepted. One day I was working at a menial job on a ship and I thought, What am I doing? I can be my own person without trashing where I came from. So I decided that when I got back to the States I was going to finish college."

I've met a lot of Roys over the years. They're the children of loving families whose only mistake was that they were "normal." Roy grew up with plenty of forgiveness, material comfort, advantages, and independence, but he felt obliged not only to pave his own path but to reject his family at the same time. Roy eventually became a teacher, and when he wrote his life story, he realized that his family had provided him with every opportunity to develop into his own person but he didn't accept what he was offered. He told the group, "I thought my family would think I wasn't good enough if I asserted myself in their presence, so instead, I behaved as if *they* weren't good enough."

Another group member, Carole, wrote that when she was in high school her father said she was so smart that if she'd been a boy he would have sent her to medical school. Her father was European-born and did not believe in educating his daughters. When she wrote her life story and described the cards she had brought to the table, she was struck by the relief she felt when she finally separated out her father's powerful words, which she had always believed meant she was inferior, and the fact that she had a family card with a particular philosophy about girls being educated. Carole enrolled in the group when she was seventy-two years old and was about to earn a bachelor of science degree.

Not all life stories are magically changed for the better after a crisis or an insight, of course. Sometimes the best prescription for progress is simply to accept your life the way it has been lived.

Audrey's earliest memory of her father was when he "slapped me awake when I was two because I wouldn't wake up fast enough." She wrote about a man who kept moving his family around, always thinking there was something better somewhere else. He never spoke to her, and she remembered being afraid of his bad temper. He was a bitter man during bitter times who treated Audrey like a burden. "If I was on my own," he always said, "I'd be better off."

Many men during the Depression behaved in this manner. Their better nature was corrupted by the uncertainty of the times in which they lived. Audrey's family card was enhanced by her mother, however, who watched over her and gave her warmth. When she wrote about her family, instead of spending a lot of time on her father, who she said was a worn-out subject, she saw how fortunate she was to have had a loving mother. But until she saw the contrast, her mother's powerful role in her life had been overshadowed by the darker power of her father.

Linda's father had grown up on the Lower East Side of New York where boys went either to jail or into show business. He never graduated from high school, and whatever dreams he might have had were dashed by the Depression. He worked hard, and he drank once a year on New Year's Eve.

And that's all she really knew about his background until she wrote her life story and made connections between how this hardworking, honest man influenced so many branching points in her life. Even though he had died a decade earlier, by writing her life story she felt closer to him than ever before. I'm always amazed, even when a parent has passed away, at how much you can learn about him or her by looking back at your own life.

> *How would you describe the kind of family you were born into? How would you describe that same family today? Was there one specific characteristic of your family that still influences you?*

When people write about their lives in a group, they are

impressed not only with what others have gone through but also by all that they themselves have survived. I'm also impressed with how group members help one another to be more understanding of family frailties. I have seen so many people shift emotional gears from "poor me" to "praise me" after simply reviewing other events that they have overcome. The change of emphasis from victim to victor is about getting a more balanced picture of your life rather than trying to recover from cards dealt to you at birth that you had no power to control.

Siblings certainly have no control over their birth order or how their parents treat them as individuals. How did your parents react when you were hurt by a sibling?

Were you the oldest child? The youngest? What was that like? What were your parents' expectations? What were some of your early experiences with justice? How were infractions of the rules handled?

My brother Raymond was two years older, taller, and stronger than I was, and he treated me as a required annoyance during our growing-up years. I suffered a lot of humiliations from him. Only when I started my adolescent growth spurt did he tolerate playing with me in the same football games. By that time I was used to the idea that I was the tolerated shrimp. I did reach six feet by the time I stopped growing, but he topped me by two inches.

Recording your life helps to assuage some of the pain. It helps us to see that most parents are frail humans who tried to make sense of things and did what they thought was right with the information they had collected.

Since we are no longer children, it makes no sense to continue to hold our parents accountable for everything that is wrong in our lives. There is no escaping how powerful they were in influencing our early lives. But with introspection, you will realize that parents can be just as valuable as negative models as they are for positive ones.

My father, for instance, had a nasty temper. I clearly saw how that temper got in the way of his success. Rather than bemoan what an angry man he was, I chose, as an adult, to see anger as something of a red flag for myself.

I think by the time you're an adult you realize that you possess some of your parents' strengths and weaknesses. It makes sense that the two people who together contributed all of your essential characteristics and then went on to raise you in an environment they created would make an enormous impression on you.

The simplest of family activities provide the richest material. Even if your parents never told you a thing about themselves or weren't modern enough to seek family therapy, all you have to do is remember back to when you were a child sitting down for family dinner.

One woman remembered how every meal was punctu-

ated with an argument between her parents. One man recalled that he had the same dinner of steak and salad for
ten years. Linda remembered how her mother would buy
one hot dog and cut it in half for her and her brother. She
would wolf hers down only to be tortured by watching her
brother eat his in slow, tiny bites. Entertainer Joan Rivers
jokingly remembered her mother's china pattern as a skull
and crossbones. Her punishment "was being sent to bed
with dinner." And writer Calvin Trillin on the subject of
mealtime said that "the most remarkable thing about my
mother is that for thirty years she served nothing but left-
overs. The original meal has not been found."

I often use the family dinner table scene as a way to
recall long-forgotten memories:

1. Did you have fixed places at the dinner table?
2. Where did you sit?
3. Where did the other members of your family sit?
4. If your father wasn't home for dinner, who sat in his
   place?
5. Was talking encouraged?
6. Was it a time to review the day and bring up the faults
   of children for an accounting?
7. Who set the agendas for table talk?
8. Who usually dominated dinner conversation?
9. What were your favorite meals? Least favorite?

10. Where did you eat the family meal? What was on the table?
11. Who did the cooking in your house, and what do you remember most about mealtimes?
12. Did mealtime change as you got older?

I don't know a living soul whose childhood was completely satisfying, but I've met many who felt loved and cared for and protected as well as some who didn't.

Money

Poker, for the most part, is a game of chance. You keep certain cards and throw others back. You bet money on the hope that you can improve your hand. And then you bet again after you put the new cards in place. Which ones do you discard? Do you bet with a bad hand? How much do you bet with a good hand? What happens if you throw the whole hand in

> *What did you like about the hand you were dealt in life? What did you dislike most about the hand you were dealt?*

and start over? For a long time, your betting power was determined by others while you sat at the table and listened to their decisions. Throughout your life you will have many hands to play and many questions to answer, but like everyone else, you had an original situation from which you learned about money.

I told you about my birth and how my father rolled dice to raise the money to pay the hospital. Money was always a very chancy thing with him. My mother always worried that we wouldn't have enough. As a result, my brother and I grew up between a passive frightened mother and a father who moved in and out of jobs trying to earn a stable income. But I don't remember being in need. Attitudes about money, not the quantity, left their impression on me and made me worry.

The Depression impressed on me the value of money and the unhappy situations people can get into without it. There was no unemployment insurance in those days. From my father I learned that there was always a way to earn a few dollars, and from my mother I learned how to save it. She saved money in a teapot. She always worried about having enough to buy things that were dictated by the times, like new suits for Easter. From her I learned how a few coins could add up when you really needed cash. My first recollection of money was about at age six when my parents gave my brother and me a weekly allowance of ten cents. My mother urged us to put part of it away to teach us the value of saving. I put mine in a little wooden chest.

Linda remembers getting a nickel every time she practiced the piano. Once she broke open the bank and tried to see whether there were enough nickels in the bank to cover her from head to foot. Her mother took all the money away. From that point on, all her childhood earnings came from the sale of Kool-Aid and old comic books. She had a lot of enterprises, but she never learned to save.

I also had a lot of enterprises. I remember buying cartons of cigarettes at a discount and then selling the individual packs to my father at market rate. I made a quarter profit per carton every week. By the time I was fourteen, my brother and I both had savings accounts held by the local post office. These accounts paid about 2 percent interest, and they didn't fail during the Depression.

My father was a risk-taker. When he wanted to buy four acres of vacant land he borrowed several hundred dollars from my brother and me—the savers. He bought the land at the end of a period of prosperity and had to wait ten years for the property to recover its value. But he did repay us, and from that experience I learned more

> *What did you learn about money when you were growing up and from whom did you learn it? Whom did you ask for money? When you were given your cards of life how many chips were piled in front of you and what were you told about them? What kind of childhood enterprises did you have? What did you do with the money?*

about saving than about risk-taking. I'm still slow to take cash out of my pocket.

Home

Just the word "home" conjures up memories and feelings about the rooms where events of your life took place. I can remember the toilets that were frozen during cold Illinois nights and the sight of lights flashing in my window when I was still in my crib.

My first memory is being in a crib in my parents' bedroom. And then I can remember sharing a room with my brother. We never had separate rooms, so, for me, the thought of home brings up a feeling of being crowded.

What is the first room you remember?

I've met many people who felt compelled to return to their childhood home. Their memories returned as they walked through the neighborhood they grew up in or along the route they followed to school or when they sat in the room where they had once slept.

Did you grow up in a male or female home?

For others, the memory of an object will unlock their emotions. Lucy's account of her home in a small midwestern community was dominated by her three older brothers.

Her memory was less about specific rooms and more about the sight of footballs, basketballs, and shotguns throughout the house. It was very much a male home, from her perspective. Remembering all that sporting equipment, she also recalled how much of her youth had been spent in a balancing act between working hard at being strong and athletic like her brothers and expressing her femininity by dressing up and using makeup.

I grew up in a male household, where my mother softened the atmosphere with her quiet voice. There were a lot of tools. My father rented a small bungalow in Chicago with two bedrooms and an unfinished basement that housed a large coal bin and a boiler for heating the house.

I can remember when nine tons of coal were delivered and dumped through an open window into the bin below. The basement was strictly a male domain where my brother operated a ham radio station. It was my responsibility to clean up the coal dust—the price I paid to get attention from my brother.

Home meant responsibility for cleaning, something my wife appreciates. But I

Who cleaned your home? Is your home in order now? Who's in charge of creating order?

gather from listening to other people's life stories that cleaning is a chore with no end that most people try to get out of. For me it was an act of accomplishment which, in my youth, had major consequences. If I didn't do a good job, I couldn't operate the ham radio with my brother. Simple cause and effect.

I didn't get a good map of my future from growing up in Chicago in a first-generation family. My parents were trying to get along one day at a time. Not too much was expected from me. Although I used to think I could use some help, I think I did better by not having parents hovering over me. I had to work harder in college to make up for what I consider a weak beginning. We all have an early history. Mine isn't terribly dramatic or unusual. My history lesson was that I felt I had to make my own life—starting with filling out my own birth certificate.

> *What were your history lessons?*

However your history unfolded, no matter what cards were dealt out in your hand of life, the task was the same: to make something of yourself. I'm not sure anyone has ever received a perfect hand.

CHAPTER 3

How Did I Play the Hand I Was Dealt? ⤴

IN the last chapter we talked about an imaginary poker game where you were dealt a hand of cards. The game began, but your original hand was not of your own choice and you played by rules made up by people who held the trump cards: food, clothing, shelter, love, and money. At some point in the game of life you hold your own cards and experiment with who you are.

> *How did you play the hand you were dealt? When did your childhood end? When did you feel you were taking care of yourself? When did you first feel accountable? What was the first decision you made for yourself?*

I don't think I've been a high-risk player so much as a strategic player. My approach has been to extract as much emotion as possible from a situation before I make a decision. I tend to make up my mind slowly. From my father I learned that hot-tempered decisions are a losing approach.

> *How active were you in making decisions for yourself? Did your decision-making most resemble your father's style or your mother's? What was the best decision you made for yourself?*

My mother's style was passive; she let life happen to her. So I grew up between two approaches, neither of which seemed suitable for my future.

I think my single best move was staying in school. During my junior year of college I was befriended by two professors, one a psychologist and the other a teacher of art. Up to that point I was suspicious of outsiders. I had a "don't tell, don't expect" attitude, which was the residue of my mother's "the more people know about you, the less they like you" view of the world.

When psychologist David Kopel helped me, I was genuinely surprised. He asked me to tutor a small boy with a reading problem and later arranged for me to take a volunteer job in the psychology department at Elgin State Hospital.

The art teacher, Arthur Fallico, encouraged me to start a philosophy club. At first I said no. I was self-conscious about my early education. At the same time, though, I wanted to prove myself wrong about not being up to the task. Organizing and leading a group forced me out of an adolescent shell I probably would have carried around for a much longer time.

Those two teachers sought me out and offered me opportunities where I could learn about myself in relation to other people. For someone like me, who thought that my only hope of success lay in my own perseverance, the transition from being a loner to becoming someone who accepted help from others was a critical part of my journey. The most important feat was conquering the fear that accepting help from others meant losing some of what I had already accomplished on my own. For reasons I can only attribute to my background, I felt that whatever I accomplished with the help of others wouldn't be entirely mine.

> *What kind of bets have you made on yourself? What did you invest? Whom did you ask to invest with you? What experiences influenced the way you played your hand? What bets didn't you make?*

I have heard fears like these expressed over the years by people who came from modest backgrounds. They played their hand by taking few risks, keeping their cards close, and holding on tight to their winnings. But often the same people regretted not having taken more chances on themselves. I think the real gamble in this imaginary card game is betting on yourself.

Some people play the game only to win. Others play to overcome the odds, real or imaginary. I know some people like my mother who sit waiting to see how the hand plays out. Others take an early loss and drop out of the game of life entirely. Some commit social suicide and stop caring about themselves. Some drop out temporarily.

When life delivers a catastrophe, there are few alternatives. A family loses its money and the children have to drop out of school and take menial jobs. A tornado demolishes the family home and temporary housing is secured away from a child's school and friends. Illness of a parent suddenly puts pressure on the oldest child to be a caregiver. Life stops for the time being. And we repeat the line from Samuel Beckett, "I can't go on. I'll go on."

Were you caught in any ups and downs of your family? How was your initiative harmed or helped? Did your life return to its earlier status? How did it change?

After a while, depending on how many times you bet, you understand you're not going to win every time. And when you don't, your recovery from defeat becomes a source of strength for the next round in the competition. Confidence comes from actual achievement as well as from the knowledge that you are a contender, someone who's ready for the competition.

Remember that poignant scene from *On the Waterfront* when the has-been boxer character, Marlon Brando, confronts his mob-connected brother? In a fight that was fixed in favor of his opponent, he was robbed not of winning but of his right to be a contender. "I could have been a contender, Charlie," he tells his brother. "Instead, I am a bum."

Anyone who has ever played poker knows you need good cards to last until the end. Waiting for opportunities to play might mean sitting out a few hands, which is quite difficult to do without giving up hope that you're still in the game.

Sometimes the rules change without notice. Jessie was surprised when her company was sold and all of the employees were advised that they were being transferred to the Midwest. She had been promoted to vice president only two months before and had a big future with the company, but she didn't want to leave California. She thought of Minnesota as a foreign country—the same way she had thought of the United States when she arrived from Eastern Europe as a child. She joined my autobiography group at the suggestion of a friend who had recently finished telling her life story. The friend recognized Jessie's branching-point situation.

Jessie told the story of how her family had immigrated to America when she was eight years old. Her parents had no money, and they moved in with relatives. There were nine people living in two rooms, and she remembered being told what to do by strangers.

"Every minute of my life was regulated by people who had no real interest in me," Jessie said. As soon as she wrote about that part of her history, she recognized that her job transfer was bringing up that childhood feeling of impotence.

She knew she had two conflicts with the same theme: starting over. She could keep her job and move to a new place or stay in familiar surroundings and get a new job. She decided that where she lived was more important to her than where she worked, and she took a silver hand-shake from her company and set out to find a new job. She didn't look back, and four months later she found a good job.

The need for change has to make itself known to the person. Your life talks to you through your experiences. Jessie's autobiography gave her the message in a picture from her past when she was a little girl with no choices.

She had been paralyzed by circumstances then, but she now was free to move forward.

Sometimes you have to wait a long time and endure a lot of losses before you cash in. Sometimes, when you think you've been outplayed, you throw in your hand before the game is over.

The idea of luck just didn't sit right with me, because if I believed in good luck I would be compelled also to believe in bad luck. For me, it's all about timing and circumstances: knowing when to act and when not to act, and understanding where I fit in the present or future needs of society. I believed in the luck of possibilities, but unlike my mother I didn't wait for life to open doors for me.

> *Did you follow the rules or break them? How did you deal with success and failure? What skills did you most rely on? What experiences did you have with waiting?*

To benefit from new possibilities, you can't be so entrenched in what you're doing that you miss the radar signals that might alert you to a new direction. I think you have to know what's going on in your field and keep moving forward.

For example, when I was heading up the groundbreaking Program on Aging of the National Institute of Child

Health and Human Development, I had three children ranging in age from nine to eighteen. My family was happy living in the Maryland suburbs, but I had to borrow money on my G.I. life insurance policy to send my oldest child to college. I was borrowing from my future rather than investing in it.

When the University of Southern California recruited me to be the first director of its newly formed Institute for the Study of Retirement and Aging, my family did not want to move. But I was thinking about the future: how was I going to send my other two children to college and what was my next forward career move.

Unlike my father, I never left or stayed in a job for emotional reasons. I was attracted to positions where I was the first jobholder and could therefore create the conditions in which I worked. I played the hand I was dealt with a certain acute awareness of how my independence card could actually destroy my career. Yet I couldn't feel secure professionally unless I created the job.

> *Have you stood in your own way? What were some of your best moves?*

I found a successful way to live with my "I must do it myself" life theme. I turned over the loner coin, found its self-starter side, and created a pattern in my professional life of moving toward new problems, solving them, and making the organization operational. My essential personality never changed. I simply learned not to stand in my own way.

My best moves had a lot to do with understanding what areas in society were expanding and getting a sense of what was going to happen in the future. When students ask me to describe how to stay aware of the daily events while your mind is planning two or three years ahead, I tell them to use a telescope and a microscope interchangeably.

The decision to uproot my family and move to California in 1965 was based on short-term financial reasons and on my view of the future of gerontology, which I felt was going to become rooted in academia. When I took the position at USC, there were no gerontology schools in the world. When the Institute for the Study of Retirement and Aging expanded into the School of Gerontology a few years later, I became its first dean.

> *What went into your decision-making? Were you a farmer who planted seeds for new opportunities, or did you show up for the harvest? Were you a map reader who plotted the next move in an already explored land, or did you sketch in pencil where you might be next? How did you define success? How did you achieve success? What gives you satisfaction?*

While I was capable of making good career moves, I was not terribly good in other areas. Many of my dumb moves had to do with money. When I was in college, for example, I suggested to my father that he invest some money in Packard Motor stock. Soon after that, Packard went out of business, taking my father's savings along with it.

Later, when I had saved some money, I thought I could make a quick profit by investing in the commodities market, so I bought cocoa futures. Cocoa fell in price and I lost a large amount of money. I also lost my self-respect. I knew nothing about the commodities market, and I made a dumb move based on too little information—something that was the opposite of the way I ran my career. In my academic life, what looked like risks really were moves that didn't present any alternatives. I specialized in organizing new research programs, not in taking risks. I didn't gamble. There are other ways to take risks—in relationships, in sex, and in trusting others with our confidences.

Were you a risk-taker? In what areas of your life did you take risks? In what areas do you wish you had taken risks?

The first half of my adult life was about filling coffers with money, things, and achievements. I've come to realize that the second half is about personal fulfillment without getting snared in ideas of personal gain. I'm no longer strangled by the distractions of youth. Now that I've taken myself out of the race to get ahead, I prefer to measure myself by my own brand of personal progress.

At my stage in life I don't worry about money, I worry about getting my work done and fulfilling my obligations. I would hate to worry about money at the same time.

Take, for example, the story of two women who had given up practicing law to be wives and mothers. They met for the first time when they were both widows in their late sixties. Twelve years and ten thousand cases later they are partners in a family law center serving the working poor. Neither takes a paycheck because they were both left well off by their late husbands. What makes these two women leave their beautiful homes to work in an office with bars on the windows? They say, "The impact we have on people's lives—clients and staff." The two lawyers waited until they reached a suitable point in their lives. They were no-nonsense, seasoned professionals who probably wouldn't have considered the same type of practice earlier in their careers. They took a chance at the right time.

I believe that the first part of your life was spent in this metaphorical poker game, blessed and burdened by the hand that was dealt to you. It is your history, but it pretty much unfolded without a clear strategy. Somewhere in your depths you understood that and tried to be in control by overachieving or by not achieving or by reacting, sometimes in destructive ways, to being swept away by circumstances not in your control.

In your second fifty, the freedom to be yourself is the reward for staying in the game. Some say that the second fifty is your last chance to get your life together. I say it's your first chance.

In the first twenty-five years of your life certain ingredients were mixed together—your genetic makeup, your parents and family, the times and environment you grew up in, your health, and the quality of the love you were given. You were young, you knew little, and you had no control over these influential elements.

Then for the next twenty-five years you took an active role and added the yeast—experience—to the ingredients. You explored your sexuality and intellectual abilities. You made decisions about work and relationships and either lived with the results or made new decisions. Let's call this blending process growing up.

Now you are the sum of nature and nurture, a bread, if you will, produced from an array of ingredients. But you're by no means a hostage of your own history. You have been gifted with a long enough life to stop and think how you want to live the rest of it. I believe you have an opportunity to live an authentic life that is of your own making.

You are someone who has grown to maturity via a history of hardships and accomplishments. You can identify the branching points and examine them with a perspective that you never had when you were younger, and you are aware, after reviewing your life, that the most tragic of experiences can also produce positive results.

You are an original. No one has had quite the same life or played the hand exactly as you did or left the same fingerprints on your cards. The point is that whatever your next moves are, you will experience them as yours and yours alone.

CHAPTER 4

Who Was I Trying to Be? ⇐

You were dealt a handful of life cards. You played them. You made some good moves and made a few mistakes. How did you learn to play? When you were a young child you randomly imitated the authority figures in your life. As you grew, you found heroes with X-ray vision, hides of steel, and the ability to fly—important qualities for a little person with no real power. As you traded in and traded up many of your models, you shaped your own personality and set goals for yourself. Later, as a young adult, you found specific traits in an assortment of people whom you admired and wanted to be like. And you also saw traits that you just as passionately rejected. You were assembling the person you were supposed to be or should be. Or maybe you learned who you should be through trial and error as you wove your way through opportunities and experiences. No matter. There comes a time in your life when you take a walk. And that walk, wrote artist Willem de Kooning, is in your own landscape.

On that walk I think all of us would like to say our life is our own. My experience tells me that people quite naturally begin to question their authenticity at this point in their lives: What was I thinking when I did that? What does all my work amount to? Am I a fraud? What do *I* really want?

The playwright David Mamet remarked during an interview that he first noticed at around age fifty, after reviewing his work, that the themes of his plays took a circular route and pointed him back to his original core, which was, in his words, "a good Jewish boy." Not until he had amassed a body of work was he able to explore his core and use it as a new point of departure.

I don't think that core, as Mamet called it, is available early in life, even to artists. Those of us who are not gifted with a body of work in which to track our development can review our life stories, just as Mamet rereads his plays, and examine who we were trying to be. And after doing so, we can take that walk into the landscape of the second fifty. The point of departure is any time when you think you have gathered enough experiences to become a source of your own inspiration or maybe even a model for others.

When I was a little boy in Catholic school, I was impressed at the sight of priests wearing regal robes. In those pre-microphone days whenever a priest quoted Scripture in a voice that reverberated from every corner of the hall, I thought I was in the presence of some absolute power. I wanted to become a priest. If I'd been a playwright later on in life, I probably would have written a play about a priest struggling with right and wrong.

Competing with my priest model was my paternal grandfather, Peter, who was a carpenter. Unlike the priests, he did no talking; he used tools and made things. I used to visit him in his large wood shop in the basement of his house. When I entered his world, I was captivated by the smell of sawdust, the sight of the racks of wood and all the tools neatly hung on the wall. I thought anyone who had a haven like that and was able to make things with his hands must truly be a man of great power. I gave him a new corncob pipe and can of Prince Albert tobacco every Christmas, and I couldn't wait to smoke my own pipe, grunt out a few orders, and make furniture.

> *When you were a small child, what person did you most admire? What quality in that person attracted you —power, beauty, kindness, skill? Have any of these qualities stayed with you?*

And then books came into my life. A few years later my maternal grandfather, Frederick, moved into first place as the person I most admired. He had shelves filled with books and magazines. Whenever I visited his house, he sent me home with a stack of books. Looking back, I realize now that he was educating me by sharing his interests and encouraging me to be an explorer of ideas. He never said so, but I think, by his deeds, he hoped that I would actually get to see the world that he could only imagine while reading *Pathfinder* magazine seated in his rocking chair in Chicago.

By the time I was twelve years old I had models who influenced me in three areas: the spiritual, the craftsmanlike, and the intellectual.

My father, on the other hand, was a mixed model, as many parents are. Earlier I mentioned his bad temper as something I disliked about him and consciously avoided in myself. But when I examined the people who gave my life meaning, I understood my father's role as more than just a negative model. He never became a real model for me until I decided, when I went to high school, to become an engineer. My father wasn't educated beyond the eighth grade, but he loved learning, and by reading a magazine, he taught himself how to fly-fish. When he bought a copy of *The Handbook*

> *Can you trace your early dreams back to certain people? Did you know your father's dreams? Your mother's? Which characteristics do your models have in common?*

of Chemistry and Physics, he overreached himself. I always thought that book symbolized the science career he never had. My dream of becoming an engineer began where my father's dreams ended. Looking back, I can see how my father taught me that knowledge was the real power, and all of my models after him were people of learning.

The Great Depression was a great killer of dreams. When I saw mature men on every main street corner selling apples for a nickel and long lines of engineers standing on the unemployment lines, I changed my model person. I was scared into the security model of becoming a teacher. I had the typical dilemma of my generation: I needed more school to qualify for teaching jobs and more work to pay for school.

Did you experience something in your life comparable to the great killer of dreams? What transitions did you make? Under what circumstances did they come about?

But there were also many opportunities. I was introduced to the fledgling field of psychology by David Kopel, who encouraged me to continue my education and attend graduate school in psychology at Northwestern University.

At Northwestern, my psychology professor, Robert H. Seashore, was a fine model for me as a bridge between the engineer I had wanted to be and the psychologist I would become. He liked gadgets and invented an automatic calculator long before the days of computers. We worked well together. Using his designs, I made some psychological testing instruments that measured hand tremor and fine motor skills. For me this was a transition from "Jim the machine shop man" to "Jim the idea man."

Linda and her brother Harry grew up in an extended family of twenty-one funny and dramatic people. The men were policemen, firemen, or postal workers like their fathers. Her aunts were saleswomen. Her models came from the biographies she read of Babe Ruth, Jonas Salk, Amelia Earhart, Enrico Caruso. She didn't want to be an Amelia Earhart; she wanted to know how Earhart became outstanding. Then something interesting happened: the more she read about accomplished people, the more fascinated she became with the ways in which they handled setbacks. She credits her own perseverance and tenacity to the champion models she read about.

Harry, her brother, knew from early childhood that he wanted to be a doctor. His model was the family physician, Dr. Gallagher, a compassionate man who made house calls and brought comfort and love along with his black bag. He was the enduring model against whom Harry measured his successful medical career.

Not all models necessarily move you forward. In my thirties, a colleague, an anatomist named Isadore Gersh, who was born in the slums of New York and became a distinguished professor, had done some interesting research by blending new principles of physics with the study of cells. I liked his eclectic research technique and wanted to do some work on my own in biostatistics and aging, but I needed more mathematical skills. I sat in on a course in mathematics at the University of Chicago, which was recommended to me as a good basis for doing some new work in modern biostatistics. The small group of students were the brightest in the field. Some were prodigies still in their teens, and I was thirty-two years old. I wrote lecture notes on material I only partially understood and listened to the younger students debate with the professor about things I'd never heard of. The only thing I learned was that no matter how hard I studied or paid attention, I had mathematical limits. I had to scale down my expectations of what I wanted to get done in the mathematics of aging. My model, Isadore Gersh, taught me that I should try to stretch myself to the limit, but my experience told me to recognize where the limit was.

> *What models are with you today? What did they teach you?*

> *Did you have models who taught you your limits? How did you react?*

I wouldn't call Gersh a negative model because I wanted to follow his example, even though I learned I couldn't. When you look back at your life and discover who influenced you, it's also helpful to look at the people you felt so much disgust for that you made a strong effort to be their opposite. The anti-models are sometimes more powerful.

Jane recognized that her mother used the power of money to control her children. She was the only one of her siblings who freed herself by rejecting her mother's money. At first, when she was young, she chose a life in extreme opposition to her mother's. She sent her mother's checks back, worked at odd jobs during the day, and went to college at night. She lived in the poorest areas, assured that her mother would never come to visit. She eloped with someone she knew her mother wouldn't approve of and had two children before she was twenty-one.

In her late seventies, when Jane told her life story to an autobiography group, someone asked her if she was sorry. "My mother's millions bought things and people," she said. "If she had bought me, too, I would be unhappy today, but I led my own life and for that I am not sorry. What I regret was how much of my spirit was spent rebelling against her. I could easily have invested more in myself instead of putting so much energy into a life that was designed to oppose her. In a way, she did control me, even in my rebellion."

Linda's mother also demanded that her daughter be like her, but instead of living her life purely in opposition to her mother, she chose to design an original role for herself. Linda became the teacher her mother wanted to be, but Linda's classroom was a refuge for highly intelligent offbeat kids who were regarded as behavior problems and who had not flourished with other teachers. She created a special curriculum for the gifted but nonconforming child. She made it up on the job.

A few years ago she received a phone call from a former student who had a third grader of his own. "Do you remember me?" he asked thirty years later. Mark was the very bright but annoying little boy who'd had a habit of taking up class time by telling jokes. Linda limited him to two jokes before the first bell rang, which solved his relentless joke telling and got him to school on time. He said he still thinks of her often as the "weirdest" teacher he ever had.

Mark told her that when she restricted homework to students who wanted to be scholars, he wanted to be a scholar. He described in perfect detail the table where she had put her broken appliances so that kids who finished their work early could tinker with them and not get into trouble. He became interested in fixing things.

He reminded Linda of how she had comforted his distraught mother, who had recited Shakespeare to him when he was still in his crib, and told her not to worry about Mark's handwriting because he could always type.

Tears streamed down Linda's cheeks as she listened to this grown man, an accomplished orthopedic surgeon, repeat one anecdote after another from a chapter of her life that was closed. When he finished, he wanted to know if she could come to Texas and teach his children. "I'm not that weird anymore," she said. "I've been to graduate school."

The second fifty is the time in life when the blending process of all the models of youth naturally draws to a close and you begin to refine yourself. You relax the rules governing what you should be, especially the ones pertaining to what it means to be male or female.

> *Who were your negative models? What were the benefits? What were the costs? Did any originality emerge? What became of the originality? Did you follow the originality to any specific goal?*

After sixty years, while I was visiting Japan, touring the gardens surrounding the old emperor's palace, something artistic awakened inside me. I listened to the tour guide talk about samurai warriors sitting beside a stream at the edge of the garden. As the story goes, they wanted to drink sake, but to do so they created a contest. Each warrior had to compose a haiku that took exactly the same amount of time to read as it took for a cup of sake to float down the stream and arrive in front of them. The vision of warriors writing poetry—the ultimate blending of strength and beauty—affected me. When I returned home, I took up gardening and flower arranging.

Women in their second fifty, especially women who came of age before or during the feminist movement, might face a dilemma similar to mine. Whereas I was limited to a certain set of male models for the sake of appearing masculine, women who sought equality in a man's world incorporated few feminine models for fear of appearing weak in a male-oriented atmosphere.

In your second fifty a natural tension comes about as the landscape of your life changes. Some changes, like downsizing or watching your children leave home, are powerful reminders of how new models of behavior are required even though you may not know exactly what they are. How does a professional who performed well at his job behave when he's asked to leave a company in order to raise an arbitrary bottom line? How do parents who gave their best twenty years to raising a child behave when that child is an adult? What's the new relationship about? Where are the models?

Some of the models we have been using in our roles as workers or parents are outdated and need revision. Writing your life story and telling it in a group is the best way of getting rid of out-of-date models. Once you do that, you can release the power you have to create a second-fifty landscape you would like to live in.

The histories of who we are and what we were trying to be involve thinking about the important people in our lives, the history of our ideals, and the shaping experiences that have influenced us right up to the present. Even though we tend to become more practical as we get older, keeping some models from the past and developing new ones that fit the times we live in will help us to take those first steps into our own landscape.

Components of the Ideal Person I Wanted to Be

Write the name of the person or character from a book or film whom you used as a model.

CHARACTERISTICS	POSITIVE MODEL PERSON	NEGATIVE MODEL PERSON
Achievements		
Appearance		
Creativity		
Friendships		
Health		
Influence, power		
Money		
Originality		
Outlook on life		
Philosophy		
Religion		
Other		

PART TWO

Present:
Where
Am I?

CHAPTER 5

How Do I Feel about My Life?

THE French have a saying that who you are at forty is who you are. I can understand that thinking if you agree that human nature never changes. But what about your second nature, the part of you that is admirable, that always seems to know what's right for you? When you listen to your second nature, you are yourself, comfortable in your own skin. Maybe you call this acting on your instincts, but there is a personal voice within all of us that knows better. What's better isn't necessarily the easiest or the most instantly gratifying path, but it usually serves your best interests.

In the second fifty, with all of your experience, you finally have the seniority to turn up the power for the voice that tells you to do right by yourself. Mark Twain said that you should always do the right thing not only because you'll be more satisfied with the results but also because it will amaze others. The life review is a lot like a voice check of your emotions. Up to this point in your life story, you've learned where you've been. Now it's time to examine where you are and how you feel.

> *What's going on in your emotional life right now? What are your needs? What's missing? When do you feel most comfortable in your own skin? When was the last time you listened to your second nature? When did you not listen? What happened? When did you last take a stand on something?*

When Joel Robuchon, one of France's greatest chefs, announced at age fifty-one that he had arrived at a level where it was difficult to do any better, he said, "To continue without progress is not my style." He had mastered what he set out to do, but it no longer brought him the same satisfaction. My experience says that's healthy—a slowing down of passion signals that you need new influences in your life.

Robuchon didn't make any radical changes. He didn't abandon haute cuisine. His future plans included a cooking school and a show for French television, both projects that expanded on his expertise, brought new people and ideas into his life, and gave him a new point of departure.

My guess is that Robuchon had been stuck before he

ended his career as a chef and spent time figuring out where he was, what he needed, and how he should move forward. With reflec-
tion, he found the answers he needed, as we all can do.

When Charlie Chaplin was making the movie *City Lights,* things weren't going well, so he decided to stop the cameras. The entire

> *How do you react when your passion level drops? What do you tell yourself? What's the balance between your passion level and your satisfaction level?*

crew just stood by waiting while Chaplin, lying on the floor for what seemed like hours, figured out the solution to the scene.

It takes a lot of emotional courage to stop in your tracks and take stock. If you stop for the first time in your adult life, you too are free to express yourself or not move until you are satisfied. But you can't simply stop in the middle of a busy life and expect to find fast answers to serious questions. The first step is to get out of your own way, loosen the emotional armor you've carried around all these years, and let in a little fresh air.

It has been my experience with autobiography groups that once the armor of convention, old habits, and old fears is loosened, people become free to look clearly and honestly at their lives and then ask, "What am I going to do with the rest of my life?" Later they ask, "How can I make my life more meaningful?"

There comes a time when the need to fill all those coffers of youth—ambition, prestige, money, parental expectations—changes to a desire for self-fulfillment, which is a more private, internal process. It is at this point that I think meaning enters your life and fills the void wherever dissatisfaction has taken up residence. You begin to change what you do to make yourself content. In so doing, you re-evaluate what taking care of yourself is all about. You begin to use your second nature. If you have two loaves of bread, the poet Kahlil Gibran wrote, you sell one to buy a hyacinth to feed your soul.

When do you feel satisfied? Which people and events do you feel satisfied with? When are you pleased with yourself? When are you not? Do some people in your life take from you? Is there enough fulfillment to balance the takers?

A woman in her mid-fifties told me she was in a major transition and hadn't a clue where she was going, but in an odd way she felt fulfilled. She said, "If I were younger I'd feel panic, but now I feel as if I'm opening up and becoming available for miracles."

Her old way of reacting to conflict had been to panic if she didn't have all the answers immediately. She couldn't tolerate being the slightest bit confused; that made her feel disoriented. She fought hard to be in control and thought she was, but she couldn't understand why she was stuck. "I used to feel stupid if I didn't see the whole picture, but now, when I can stop hyperventilating, I feel relaxed, and in those moments I know everything is going to be all right. I'd like to feel that way all the time," she told the group. For her, feeling relaxed was a miracle.

I've noticed that creative people have a vitality that more defensive folks do not. They seem to use the unknown—an empty canvas, a blank page, a block of stone—with self-expression. People with no creative form of self-expression, armed only with defenses, tend to protect themselves from the unknown. Sculptor George Segal said his vitality is highest when he is doing something new.

I'll bet that Segal and the woman creating miracles will avoid what I call musty closet syndrome (MCS). It's human nature to gather a little dust of resignation from your first fifty. The thickest layer probably accumulated during the time when you were struggling with the emotional distress of childhood. We do tend to dwell on "poor me" for quite a long time, which doesn't allow for much ventilation. Adults turn resignation into acceptance and move on. Non-adults turn it into grief, grief eventually produces emotional frailty, and MCS sets in.

I think your second nature rejects an "I can't help myself"

attitude and creates a kind of counterforce that propels you forward. I've listened to people talk about how depressed they became about the changes in their physical appearance in their second fifty. You can get a little musty if you mourn your wrinkle-free days too long. Youth may be over, but I think you can be forever youthful if you express your vitality and avoid MCS. Sparks won't fly in a musty closet.

Everyone has different criteria, or coordinates, for feeling vital. As I mentioned earlier, for the past couple of years, I've organized weekly Saturday morning walks with interesting people of all ages, some of whom are regulars. I keep sparks flying for myself by asking people questions. We walk three miles into the Santa Monica Mountains every week, and I have the damnedest of times doing the two things I love: walking and talking, but only when they're done together. Recently, one of the walkers mentioned the marriage of her eighty-year-old father to a seventy-eight-year-old woman. "Why get married?" she inquired of the group. "Because marriage stands for something," someone answered, "and these two people still believe in it." What a walk and talk that was!

I've always loved fishing. When I was young, one of my good times was going fishing with my father. We barely spoke to each other, but I remember the pride I felt when I turned over the catch to my mother as we returned home.

Now I recall how I felt loved by my father because he taught me how to fish.

I've been living in California for a long time and I'm always talking about fishing, but have never gone. My wife, Betty, doesn't like fishing, and my one son who lives nearby doesn't see any point to it. Fishing has been on my list of good things to do for a long time, and I keep thinking I should do something about it rather than make excuses.

If my "to do" list is longer than my accomplishments list, I tend to feel bad about myself. At this stage in my life, that's just nonsense. I should either erase some items and make the list shorter or just get moving. Or maybe it's time I taught someone else how to fish.

> *What are some of your best times? How do you make good times happen?*

Sometimes you have to reexperience a good time from your past to understand what you're missing. Take, for instance, the woman who felt stuck in a miserable second marriage. She was too unhappy to stay and too afraid to leave. Finally she sold her diamond engagement ring and used the cash to rent a beach house and fly her adult children out to stay with her. "I gave myself what I was missing, namely love and fun," she said. "I was getting used to being without it, and my spirit was dying. When I returned home from my retreat, the contrast was so severe that I knew it was better to leave the relationship than stay with someone who was joyless. I doubt if I could have trusted my feelings enough twenty years ago to leave. I probably would have had an affair and put off growing up."

Whenever an autobiography group completes its work, a few members always comment, sometimes months later, that when they reread their life stories they became aware of an early emotional theme that still plagues them as adults. They describe it as a roadblock on an otherwise open highway. If you dis- cover you have one road-

What feelings have you gotten used to being without? How do you react when you feel deprived?

block after all you've been through, well, that's not so terri- ble. You can learn to live with the uneasiness it produces, or you can really struggle with the conflict. I don't think you help yourself by just acknowledging its existence.

For me, I still seem to be plagued by the emotional theme of doing everything for myself or not feeling com- petent. I'm working on it, though. The truth is, I feel far more competent when I do less, but do it with greater efficiency.

Recently, I had to take stock of where I was. My office files were overloaded, and we were going to move to an- other building nearer the heart of the university but with less space. What to throw out, take home, or move to the new office was the dilemma. I couldn't put my decision off any longer. The deadline for moving was two weeks off.

I fought doing it. I had saved a vast number of letters, articles, and projects from my entire career. Everything seemed too valuable to throw out. I told myself that some-day I would actually organize years of materials.

Meanwhile, I saved it all. I had to go through forty years of files. What did I discover about myself? As I plunged into my files, I found much evidence that I expected to follow up on every dream I had—only, in reality, I didn't. I had believed that I could do almost everything in my career.

Now I was faced with sorting out the dreams and realities of what I wanted to take into the future. But what to do with the letters from friends, notes about research, data from an unfinished project?

My wife, Betty, suggested that I send the important mate-rial to the archives of the Gerontology Society of America and the American Psychological Association. A brilliant idea. Once done, my files were reduced, my feelings about the past were respected, and I was free to move forward.

The whole process was amazing. I was astonished at how much I had tried to do. But by trying to do too much I did less than I might have. I learned a tremendous amount about myself by sorting out the past. I shed tears for col-leagues and friends I felt deeply about who had died. Memories of past rivalries aroused amusement now rather than the competitiveness I once harbored. I felt freer than ever before.

I am going into the future with three projects to do and very little to distract me. I will travel lighter and with fewer people, but I will get to know them better. Things and trophies have moved down on my priority list, and relationships with people have moved up. I'm not a solo anymore, but I still have the drive to get things done.

It seems to me that no matter how old you are in years, there's a tension between past emotional themes—your old roadblocks—and the desire to improve yourself. The tension relaxes when you listen to your second nature and do the right thing for yourself. Just the act of making a decision—any decision—liberates you. You may hear an old voice saying, "No! No! You've failed before," but progress is good for you, and your second nature knows that. The more progress you make, the more you know about yourself and the more you can be yourself. If the worst thing that happens to you is living with the conflict between a pesky life theme and the constant reminder that you need

What are your distractions? Have you discovered an emotional theme from your past that stands in your way? How much armor-loosening do you have to do? How light do you travel?

to run a sword through it, well, that's not a terribly high price to pay.

I'm reminded of a gifted, multilingual sixty-eight-year-old woman who was living in a run-down house in Los Angeles with a dozen stray cats and books piled so high in spots she had to climb over them. She created a newsletter in which she reviewed international cookbooks for select subscribers. She hesitated to sell subscriptions to ordinary people because she wanted an elite clientele. She called one afternoon. "Maybe it's time to give up and do something else," she said. "I can't seem to get ahead, and I can't seem to stop this downward spiral."

I told her she was already a triumph because she was doing something original, and that had to count for something. I suggested she write a list of what she loved to do and what she was doing to achieve her goals.

Ten days later she called again to say she realized she was plagued by this notion that she wanted to be associated with a cutting-edge project. All of her sacrifices revolved around the idea of being a brilliant original person who wanted recognition. She was stuck because she couldn't think her way out of this self-image and hold on to enough self-confidence to keep going.

This woman focused more on an abstract notion of intellectual validation than on how she could use her talent to make a success of her newsletter. She put too much emphasis on a vague reward. When she didn't make progress, she became stuck in a feeling of resignation that could happen at any age. It occurs when a person says, "This is all there is. I am at a dead end. I have reached my peak, and no one wants me."

I'm reminded of a good-looking, witty, successful, high-pressure salesman who for twenty years helped build a company only to find himself out of work when the company was sold. He became stuck emotionally for two years. He was diagnosed as depressed. Although he still had the same imagination that had built a company for someone else, he didn't trust his own talent without the "security" of a corporation.

Today he keeps an envelope in his desk drawer labeled "In case of [being] fired, please open." In it, he has listed his accomplishments so he won't forget how far he's come.

Many of us have a tough time getting unstuck, because we think we'll have to make a lot of changes. I say change nothing. Loosen your armor and trust your second nature —the adult inside you who wants you to do better.

My salesman acquaintance took a painful road back into himself, but he didn't break down—he broke up, and he returned whole but with looser armor, unafraid of being free. He wasn't a different person; he simply found the emotional courage to trust himself enough to open new vistas.

One of my favorite cartoons is an illustration by Mithenberg in which a scowling fish walks up an embankment out of a pond onto land. He looks over his shoulder at the disbelieving faces of his fish friends left behind swimming. The caption reads, "Because I've already said all I can say in this particular medium." Even a fish out of water can make a go of it if he believes in his own guidance system.

But there's no guarantee that listening to your second nature and conquering emotional obstacles means

> *What does being free mean to you?*

you're a terrific person capable of doing mighty deeds.

I once read a story about an Olympic athlete who came in last in the marathon. It was after dark when he finally arrived back at the arena. Someone asked him why he bothered to continue, especially after he injured his thigh. "I wasn't sent here by my country to start; I was sent to finish," he said.

When you were young and ran for the gold, you felt "less than" if you didn't win. If you won at an early age, you were faced with a need to gather more trophies. Now you pick your races carefully, set more attainable goals, and feel satisfied if you overcome the odds you once created for yourself.

When you suit up emotionally in the second fifty, you might sometimes feel like a once wonderful house that needs some fixing up. Remember you're still charming after all these years, if a bit worn at the edges. Maybe you're cobwebbed by old life themes, pained by circumstances that have diminished your spirit, a little wanting in the nurture department—giving it and getting it—but there's love in your depths, imagination in your soul, and a sturdy frame still standing after all you've been through. You're in this life to finish on a high note, and you have the voice and vitality to make sure you do.

Chapter 6

What Do I Think about Love? ⇇

In youth, love begins when two people decide to become one. As love ripens, two individuals emerge with a desire to be understood by each other. We tell each other secrets and stories from our lives. We make ourselves known, share our past, and trust that we will still be loved. As love matures, we come to rely on each other as close allies. When you tell your love story in the context of your life story you'll see the patterns of your relationships and the many ways you love. I don't think there's anything mysterious about love in the second fifty, except perhaps our capacity to express it.

Japanese feminist Chaise Kato talked about the need for an open heart and a sharp eye: "If I see a cement wall, and between the cracks I see one seed opening, it is a small, small wild life. If a seed drops out, then nature grows from that. . . . If you look for things like that, you can move your heart ten times a day, you can become a person, and you can move your heart deeply in many ways while you are learning many, many things."

What moves your heart? How do you go about understanding someone? How do you make yourself known to someone you love?

My early ideas about love centered on what I did to make the other person feel loved. If I loved someone, but that person did not feel loved by me, then what was my love about? I loved in uncomplicated times when the male role was defined by taking care of people: I provided, therefore I loved; I provided, therefore you were loved.

I grew up without ever hearing the word "love" spoken by my parents. Ironically, I have the same problem. When I say "I love you," I follow it with "Do you need anything?" My feelings usually have to be backed up with deeds.

What are your ideas about love? When did you formulate your ideas? Which idea about love have you changed?

I admit that my once uncomplicated chiseled-out male role is in need of refinishing. I still have a tough time talking about love, and I have an equally difficult time shifting from the provider role to expressing love in other ways. Betty and I have been married for over fifty years, and like many long-married couples, we have our own rhythm. We have an imaginary line that we never cross. We no longer hurt each other even if one of us needs a nudge. We usually find a way at the right moment to air a concern but not to prove a point or be right. I used to be quick to criticize and find fault, but I've learned to live with contradictions. I'm more interested in being part of a harmonious relationship than in dominating the relationship.

Len was a classic man's man in his early sixties: rugged, self-made, good-looking in a craggy way. He traveled west every summer to live and ride with a Native American family. He went for the adventure of horseback riding, and he wasn't looking for love lessons. One night as everyone sat around the

> *What acts in everyday life speak love to you? How do you alert someone that you love him or her? When was the last time you fell in love?*

campfire, a Native American woman, sitting cross-legged, grimaced. Len happened to look up at that moment and noticed that her husband got up and propped a pillow behind her. Nothing was asked, nothing was said, but Len said that something clicked inside him as he watched the husband make his wife comfortable—a simple act that lasted a few seconds. He watched for other such moments and found many. He said when the trip was over he had learned more about love than about horses. "They had this natural balance of give and take," he said. "I had to rethink my score-keeping style where I kept this running report card in my head of 'I did, she did.' "

Harry and Virginia may have fallen in love for all the right reasons. For him, it was her matzo balls; for her, his 1938 Ford coupe. Fifty-five years later, they get up every morning and thank God they have each other. Says Harry, "Marriage is not a fifty-fifty proposition; it's a hundred percent or nothing."

Performers Steve Allen and Jayne Meadows, who have been married for over forty years, said they understood *How much of your love life is your sex life?* and appreciated right from the beginning what each brought to the relationship and how valuable the contribution was to the other's well-being. They built a life together on that understanding. "There's no yard that's greener and no man that's perfect," Jayne said. As for Steve: "It helps to know you're nuts."

Harold is one of the 40 percent of people sixty-five and older who are sexually active. He told me that he is still courting his wife after fifty-two years of marriage. His life with her is "zestful," he said, and though the intimacies may be fewer, they are no longer rushed for the sake of reaching orgasm.

Harold said he felt relieved after all these years to be less oriented toward sexual performance and more attuned to sensuality. In fact, he said he felt ever youthful because of how much longer it took to attain satisfaction. "Isn't that what we always wanted when we were younger?" he asked.

> *How do you feel in the presence of someone you say you love? How do you know you're loved?*

Marie, at fifty-three, was a skilled mountain climber who had lived alone for a long time after her divorce. She was in a serious relationship when her mother suddenly died. Soon after the funeral she became disillusioned. "I was going through a crisis and he behaved as if nothing had happened," she said. "I already felt empty from the loss of my mother, and I felt even emptier in his presence. Why was I seeing this man?"

Marie wasn't prepared for what happened next. One of her hiking partners, a man ten years younger, surprised her: "James once held me for an hour when I cried. He took time off from work, and we went hiking together. He changed his plans; he asked for nothing in return. He seemed to know what I needed. At first I was thrown off balance by the intimacy because I didn't expect to feel so comfortable with him."

Three months later, while Marie was working out at her club, she said to herself: I absolutely love him. I want to spend the rest of my life with him. I've never met anyone like him before. She bought a bouquet, went to his house, and said, "James, I love you," and walked away. She remembers him looking really bewildered. A few days later he called, but the conversation was brief and his only mention of her visit was to express his surprise.

Three months after the flowers they went away together to Yosemite. Marie remembered, "We were looking at the falls, had our arms around each other, and I said, 'I love you.' There was a pause and he said, 'Me too.'" Marie told him that "Me too" wasn't good enough and that when he was comfortable saying "I love you," she wanted to hear it.

Marie felt loved by him long before he used the words. He was first a good friend and then a good lover. "During lovemaking he was eager to learn what satisfied me. Right away I knew he was special. And slowly I became aware of feeling loved by him." A year after Marie unexpectedly gave James the flowers she asked him to marry her, and he said yes immediately.

I have heard many life stories about love. And the question I continue to ask myself is this: if we can mature in so many other ways in our second fifty, why can't we mature in the way we express love? Writing and sharing the story of your love life focuses attention on your experiences and unresolved problems with past relationships, but it does so within the context of your entire life. Everything in your second fifty is about finding expanded meaning in your life. Why not love? I think your capacity for love has yet to be measured and requires daily expression in whatever form brings you happiness. The Sufi poet Rumi wrote, "If you desire an embrace, just open your arms. If you crave a living face, smash the stone face."

How's your love life? Do you have an open heart? Are you still learning many

> *What is it that you feel when you feel loved? When was the last time you felt loved?*

things? Do you anticipate what you don't know? For someone to get really close to you, does that person have to be stuck with you in your spot with your memories and your old love habits? Or do you make new love memories?

Tom, now in his fifties, wrote that falling in love with his wife-to-be was strongly mixed with an obsessive sexual urge: "My beloved and I were so much alike; we liked the same foods, we enjoyed the same activities, we thought the same thoughts. She was a goddess, perfect in every way, and I was her knight in shining armor. When we fell out of love, as all couples must, sooner or later, I was disillusioned, and so was she. The fantasy was that we were alike and perfect, but we had to grasp the reality that we remain two different and imperfect individuals."

Tom and his wife received counseling and eventually made the conscious decision to love each other, which freed them to become truly loving and truly intimate. They argue, but underneath all of the discord is the commitment to love, which they made with an awareness of how much they need each other. This decision is the glue of their tenderness, devotion, and affection.

I remember a twice-divorced woman in her fifties who told her love stories and, at the end, wrote that she had evolved from a romantic to a realistic romantic: "I may never intimately share my life with anyone again but I think I'd know how if I did. I can face the reality that no man is perfect if he can handle that he's as flawed as me. I'm not afraid of a broken heart if he can admit he needs me."

Another woman, also in her fifties and twice divorced, told one unsatisfying love story after another. She too was resigned that she would never have a love relationship with a man, but she didn't want to live out her second fifty without the company of someone she could touch, laugh with, and share her life with. She met a woman whom she felt compatible with and for the first time established the intimacy she had always craved. "I feel loved and cherished and understood for the first time," she said, "and I cannot ignore that or deny the ultimate fact that I am happy."

When you tell your life story about love, you are making yourself known through the love experiences you've lived through and the lessons you've learned from them. Ask yourself how you love, how you want to be loved, and what you do that's loving. If you keep an open heart and a sharp eye, I think you can also learn many things by providing opportunities for others to act in a loving way. Your capacity for love has yet to be measured.

CHAPTER 7

How Do I Balance My Life Portfolio?

In Aesop's fable, the hare challenges the tortoise to a race because he's convinced that he can beat the tortoise with his speed. The tortoise's strategy is to run the race as he runs his life—by planning ahead and wasting no time. The hare makes one fatal error on his way to victory: he spends his winning margin napping while the steady tortoise quietly passes him by on his way to the finish line.

The second fifty is a time to see how you invest the time of your daily life and where you are in relation to where you want to go. I believe how you spend your time is equally as important as how you spend your money. Imagine that you have a life portfolio where your holdings or investments in the important aspects of life are recorded. I encourage you to look inside at the listings with the same kind of scrutiny that you would use to review your financial portfolio or your checkbook register.

Your answers to these questions and others are the holdings you have accumulated in your portfolio. In the second fifty, a review of how you spend your time seems natural. Once you understand how you spend time, you might want to invest differently.

If you're like most people, you need to shift the balance of your portfolio to yield better returns. For instance, Jack decided that he wasn't going in to work an hour before everyone else anymore. He was going to use the time to jog with his son.

Roberta very deliberately began evaluating how much time she spent with friends. She said, "If I was giving more than I was getting from the relationship, I would spend less time with the person."

> *Is your portfolio balanced? Do you get satisfying returns on your time investments? Are you diversified? What absorbs you creatively? Artistically? Romantically? In nature? How do you spend your Sundays? How much time do you spend having fun? What do you do that is purely unselfish?*

I remember John, a Wall Street municipal bond salesman who had made a career change to television broadcasting, entered a second marriage, and embraced city life. On the surface he had the ideal life, but one day he asked a psychiatrist friend for the name of his toughest colleague for therapy. John told me, "I began to realize that life is precious, but I was unable to balance that realization with how I was living. I spent several months cutting loose the bulk of the boat anchors I had been carrying around." When John balanced his portfolio in our autobiography group he listed his assets in the following order: "my wife, children, work, and recreation." What had begun as a vague sense that he was missing something in his life ended with a reinvestment strategy that was equitable.

Susan had a rewarding career, a good marriage, and wonderful children. In her late thirties, her husband told her that he didn't want to be married anymore and that he wanted to live with another woman. Susan recalled, "He was willing to spend half his time with me and half with her. If I wanted to continue our relationship, it would have to be in that form." Cold as it may sound, Susan's husband offered her a deal with no concessions: She had to decide whether to accept the offer or leave behind a major investment that had gone bad—her marriage. For her the choices were clear, but no matter what her decision she would be at risk. The question for Susan was, which risk was worth taking? She decided to shift her life investments to something she might win—financial independence—rather than hold on to something she already had—a compromised marriage. She invested in her future by completing her graduate education.

I don't believe that in the second half we get more conservative and avoid taking risks, but experience does lead us to estimate the odds a little more closely. We begin to rely more on the advice of others, personal experience, available information, and a greater understanding of our own needs before we make shifts in our life portfolio. So if adults appear to take longer to make up their minds, well, it's true, because for most major decisions they have a bigger inventory of experiences to review.

When I ask my autobiography groups what they would like to invest in next, some answer that they would like to play a musical instrument, learn to write well, or become public speakers. Most of these ideas seem like private dreams filed in the undeveloped portfolio category: "Someday I'll get around to it."

When I ask, "Why don't you just do it?" many answer that they don't try to find new ways to invest because of the fear of not being good enough. They would rather keep dreams alive inside than risk exposure.

Linda took the law school admittance test when she was forty. She remembered hearing other students' test booklet pages outswishing hers by two to one. She acted on her dream of becoming a lawyer but too much time had passed for her to be competitive. She was relieved to carry one less dream around.

I remember when I decided to make my transition into the computer age. At seventy-two, I was self-conscious about being a techno-peasant. I stumbled through computerspeak with salespeople, consulted my younger colleagues about their computers, and made my debut on the next technological stage by buying a computer. The gain of freeing myself of the old typewriter outweighed the risk of exposing how dumb I was about computers. But if I hadn't felt as outdated as my typewriter, I wouldn't have made the investment to learn how to use a computer. The point is that I made an objective appraisal of the value of a computer, but I also paid attention to my feelings when I shifted investments.

For many, feelings about the gain-loss ratio can result in not trying new investments. There is no reason to walk away from long-standing investments if they are sound and paying off in terms of our life goals. But investments can dry up or suddenly change. Your children leave home or move back, your job gets boring or you get downsized, your spouse retires or passes away.

When we were younger, our life portfolios had a personal investment plan that kicked in whenever life made demands on us. We invested automatically in school, career, family. Most likely, our portfolios reflected a heavy investment of time under the "I have to" category with little emphasis on a strategy for the future.

Investments in your second fifty need to be carefully thought out, and the only person who can do that is you. You are the expert. The first step is to determine where your portfolio is unbalanced.

After assessing mine I devised a graph of my present investments and then adjusted them to a future level of how I wanted to spend my time. The largest cut in time was in the work area, and the biggest increase was with people.

> *What would you be willing to do less of in order to receive a greater return?*

The professional athlete, the actor, the Nobel Prize—winning scientist, and the best-selling writer can have a narrow life portfolio with investments focused on one dominating talent. Sometimes their status translates to others investing in them but not the reverse. Relationships are tipped in one direction, and after a career decline life is lonely.

Not all public figures we read about have unbalanced portfolios. Some understand the nature of celebrity and prepare by insulating themselves from the inevitable downward turn. Norman Lear has a permanent place in the history of television as the producer of *All in the Family*, in which he made entertainment meaningful and political

My Life Portfolio: Present and Future Investment

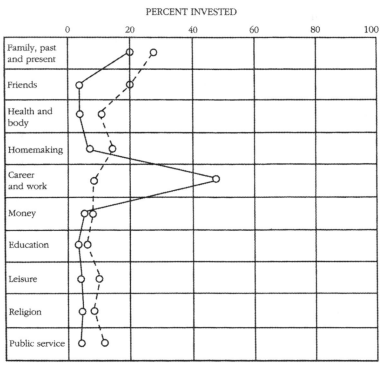

PERCENT INVESTED

○———○ Present Life Portfolio   ○– – – –○ Future Life Portfolio

without missing a laugh. But show business wasn't his whole life. During his days as number one, he invested financially in the dreams of others and created People for the American Way, an organization that monitors the Right

Your Life Portfolio: Present and Future Investment

Your life portfolio is the distribution of your time, energy, and concern with different areas of your life. This graph is designed to give you a picture of the way you have distributed your life investments and the way you may wish to redistribute them in the future.

Think of having 100 chips each worth 1 percent of your capacity to invest yourself. Each of the two life portfolio distributions, present and future, should total 100 percent, since that is your full life.

Put two dots in each category showing your present and your desired future distribution of your life investments. It is best to sketch them in pencil first so you can erase and change them as you think about them. When you finish putting in the dots, connect them with two separate lines, one for the present and one for the future. You may wish to use different colors for the lines to contrast them.

PERCENT INVESTED

	0	20	40	60	80	100
Family, past and present						
Friends						
Health and body						
Homemaking						
Career and work						
Money						
Education						
Leisure						
Religion						
Public service						

Wing Fundamentalist movement. When his career in television ended, he easily shifted his investments and continues to be an active player in society.

One wise woman I talked with about her life had raised a family and worked for charitable causes. She said she had been on the Broadway stage when she was a teenager. Her father would watch her performances from the front row balcony and later give her his critique. I asked her why she left the stage after such a strong start. "I decided my talent was not big enough for me to put my whole life into my career," she said. Early in her career she estimated the gains and losses from building a life around her talent—a very adult thing to do. Instead she chose a married life with a balanced portfolio of husband, children, and community.

We all know the more typical scenario for actors: going from one bit part to another; suffering years of rejection, deprivation, lost relationships, neglected children; and finally, maybe ten or fifteen years later, in a state of despair, calling it quits. Or maybe the phone just stops ringing and there's no decision to make.

An unbalanced portfolio has no cushion for those times when your life develops a gap or, worse, a crash. Gaps occur in everyone's life, and when they do, the void can either suck your self-esteem into it or be filled by a backup from your diversified life portfolio.

A man in one of my autobiography groups told me, "The

most important thing that happened to me was getting fired from my job. When I look back, it seems as if I was with the company forever and had my head in the sand. After I got over the jolt of not having a job, I began to realize how long I had been drifting. Being fired was a wake-up call. I am so much better off now."

Our life investments give meaning to our daily lives and provide strong emotional ties. It's only when we begin to shift investments that we feel just how strong these ties are.

Does your life portfolio have heavy investment in your career? Your physical attractiveness? Your public image? Your athletic ability? Where are your other investments?

Marilyn and Dave were married nine years, had two young children, and lived in the suburbs. Marilyn had put Dave through law school, and he'd opened his practice five minutes from home. He even played with the children during his lunch break. Then suddenly Dave announced that he had taken a job in the city with a corporation. When the entire relationship changed overnight, Marilyn felt that her partnership had dissolved and that she had been cut loose. Up to that point, she had been part of every decision made in the marriage.

Dave no longer saw his children during the week. He left early in the morning for the city and returned home after they had gone to bed. He traveled. Marilyn was isolated with the children during the week and used the weekends, when Dave was home, to escape and do things on her own. Within a year, both were having extramarital affairs, and eventually they divorced. Marilyn and Dave did not protect the equity they had invested in their relationship and their children. Their investment lost its value, and they lost everything.

> *What do you contribute to someone else's life? What are the returns? What do you need to do to get more out of your investments?*

Take some time and evaluate how you distribute your energy. Once you've done that, look at the investment and ask yourself how much value it has in your life. Does it bring you happiness? Do you feel enriched because of it? Can you grow with it?

Of all the things in autobiography, examining how you spend time every day is the least complicated. Managing your own time, though, is difficult. The shift from "I don't have enough time" to "How should I spend my time?" and how you answer that question will have a major effect on your future well-being.

The second fifty is a beginning. You have more control over your daily life than ever before. You can collect dividends on past investments. You can reinvest yourself by looking over your old portfolio, saying good-bye to worn-out investments, and paying closer attention to the durables. And then, once you've established yourself as the manager of your portfolio, you can look around for new growth investments.

PART THREE

Future: Where Am I Going?

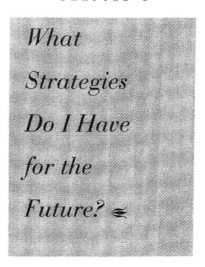

CHAPTER 8

What Strategies Do I Have for the Future?

MY autobiography groups have shown me that the walls we build around ourselves to meet the demands of every-day life are sometimes so high that we resist finding new ways to explore and develop. Long after those walls are even necessary, we forget to take them down. How can we soar to new heights if we can't surmount our self-imposed barriers?

Imagine that you are asked to choose what you like about yourself and your life and to pack all of those things into a suitcase to take with you into the next century. What will you put into storage? How much space will you leave open for your future?

Earlier I likened you to a loaf of bread—fully formed, baked, and ready, a combination of ingredients that included your genetics, childhood, adolescence, and coffer-filling years, all mixed together over a forty-year-plus period. The second fifty is about adding mastery, fulfillment, completion, expansion, meaning, and a little jam to your bread.

In the business world a company that has realized its full growth is thought of as stale unless it diversifies. It needs a new infusion of ideas or it gets crusty, even moldy. I think life without some thought about the future is a kind of stagnation that is barely felt but has huge consequences.

There's a timeless quality, a dead center, to a life without curiosity. No matter what your age, if you're living without curiosity you're in a holding pattern called coping. You're self-imprisoned. You're in a rut. You're doing 40–60 without any possibility of improvement. Coping is what you do from day to day to get by at a minimum level. It's a response to crisis. I remember trying to comfort a woman who had taken time off from her law practice to nurse her dying brother. "Taking care of a sick person must be hard on you," I said. "No, not really," she answered. "I did what was necessary and never thought about anything except making him comfortable. That's not hard." When the crisis was over, she stopped coping and returned to her daily life, which was rich and complicated and full of challenges.

Many times I'll ask people how they're doing and they'll reply: "I'm surviving." Surviving? Surviving is what you do to get through a catastrophe. You live life embattled, swords drawn, ready for combat, because you're threatened by war, starvation, or economic ruin. In some circumstances living on the barricades makes sense. But it makes no sense to live that way every day, inhaling and exhaling, waiting for the next catastrophe to happen.

Most theories in the psychology of personal development come from professionals who have treated people who couldn't meet the demands of their lives. Today we use terms like "coping strategies," "defense mechanisms," and "post–traumatic stress disorder" to characterize people as if they were castles under siege.

Theories of personality development tend to place no emphasis on techniques of expanding a life. Our approaches to understanding the human personality have been based on the study and treatment of people who needed help because they were succumbing to the problems of living. We need two strategies—one to protect our daily survival and one for creative expansion and thinking our way out of old fears.

Laura Huxley, widow of Aldous, said that for every hour of psychotherapy people receive, they should give one hour of themselves to someone else. Her idea of taking in and giving out is not as idealistic as it sounds. There comes a point, it seems to me, at which an excess of psychological self-knowledge becomes a defense in itself. It's like saying, "This is why I feel and behave in a certain way—take it or leave it." Laura is challenging the emotional isolation that results from too much self-reflection.

Eighty-five is the age that I always thought would be my last year on earth, but I charted my life to age ninety. A good number, double what I would have lived to at the turn of the last century. Seven years from now, my sense is that I will close my personal history book, which I hope will still be a work in progress.

Knowing full well that there is no perfect future or, for that matter, a predictable one, I still think it's important to imagine what your personal perfect future would be. Whether I live seven more years or fifty more years, I think the questions I must answer about my future will be the same. How do I want to end up? With whom? Doing what?

I was once in the high Sierra on a backpacking trip, and at the end of the day we sat around the campfire and I asked the group what they would do if they suddenly had a million dollars.

One of the hikers, a professor of botany, said, "Why should I wait? Why don't I live as if I had it in the bank now?" He believed that freedom, not money, was the real issue. "The question you should ask," he said, "is how would you live your life if you were truly free." The next time I heard from him, he told me that he took himself out of the tenure track and began spending only half of his time at the university. He bought a vineyard, something he had planned to do when he retired twenty years later, and spent the other half of his time growing grapes and learning the wine business.

> *When you think about the future, what do you imagine?*

When our children and grandchildren gather with us on New Year's Eve, we have a midnight ritual of "burning the bad." Each of us writes a private list of all the bad things of the past year that we would like to get rid of. When we're done, we crumple them up, put them in a ceramic bowl on the hearth, and put a match to them.

Recently we added a new ritual. Our younger son, Bruce, and his wife, Susan, pointed out that life is not only about getting rid of the bad but also about recognizing the good we have experienced. Susan made each family member a personalized Christmas tree ornament that opened up; inside these ornaments we put lists of the good things that had happened during the year. So now we focus on recognizing the good on Christmas Day, and on New Year's Eve we get rid of the bad. I think we need another holiday on which to list our wishes and goals for the future. July Fourth might be a good day for that—a day for declarations of independence and intentions for the future.

Your vision of the future changes many times during your life. When you were a child you used to say, "When I grow up I want . . ." Then when you grew up, you said, "In five years I want to achieve . . ." And then a little later, you said, "When I have the time, I want to . . ." The more autobiographies I read, the more I believe that the people who set early goals and hit them are the rare ones. I suppose most of the people I've met in autobiography groups were information-seekers. They assumed there was more to know about themselves, and they joined a group to explore their experiences and goals and to set strategies for the future. Some never discovered what they were searching for but kept an open mind just in case. People with open minds always seem to need room to expand. They are not necessarily gifted people—many, in fact, are quite ordinary—but they are acutely aware that the second fifty requires a new kind of balancing act.

I read a lot about going back to school in the second fifty. Although upgrading a worn-out diploma is probably a good idea, I think it's only half of a good idea. There are also many programs around the country that tap into the talents of retired professionals. That's half of a good idea, too. Why not combine the two in a new kind of education where you can explore yourself as a human being and give what you know to others?

Here's what a forty-five-year-old academic wrote about

his second fifty: "I have very few specific notions about my situation. But for several years I have been exploring myself, my possibilities, discovering new dimensions in my life. I have started painting, dancing, counseling, and learning to enjoy the new things this brings to me. It's a way of making the maximum out of my life now—not so much in material output but in a new spiritual approach. I am also trying to share as much as possible of what I'm doing with colleagues."

You reach a point in the process of autobiography when you have sifted and found those nuggets of personal resources. It's like panning for gold. You have to go through a lot of sludge to find those shiny little pebbles. What do you do with them once you find them? Put them in a scrapbook? Frame them and hang them up as trophies? Or convert them into some future currency?

Over the years I've observed in my autobiography groups both a formal and a casual process that I call conversion. People convert either their talents or their deficits into something more fitting as part of their expanding future.

For instance, a doctor friend who was a successful surgeon decided after thirty years to leave medicine. "My passion was diminished by the demands of the business that is now health care," he told me. Looking back at his life, he remembered a sculpture class he had enjoyed during his undergraduate years. He remembered the passion he felt when he shaped a block of marble into an object of beauty.

During the three years he spent winding down his medical practice, he built a studio where he worked every night after seeing patients. He eventually sold his practice and devoted himself to developing the part of him that was an artist. He tapped into the same intensity he'd used in becoming a doctor. One of his statues now stands in a building at UCLA. When a former colleague asked him how he liked retirement, he replied that he wasn't retired, he was reactivated.

All of my life goals and career goals, beginning when I left the town where I'd grown up to enter the navy, were about giving myself independence. Now I'm converting some of that independence into a strategy for the future. I don't have concrete goals, but I do want to expand and mature socially, morally, professionally, spiritually, and sexually and maintain a warm, comfortable home for my family and friends to enjoy during the remaining years of my life.

My mother and father retired to a small house in Saint Petersburg, Florida, where they lived a modest life on my father's Social Security and a little savings. As survivors of the Depression, they did quite well in getting a few new things they liked into their days—Gulf fishing, a dog, and a garden. But things happen. Not too long after they moved, my father developed lung cancer.

I mention this because there's no single map, no magic formula or strategy, that fits all and is permanent. From my experience I've learned that people who continued to expand their emotional or professional lives into their second fifty did little planning but placed a great deal of importance on being able to analyze and take advantage of opportunities that came their way. They knew enough about themselves to recognize what would give them the most satisfaction. They seem to balance the explorer with the navigator in them.

I remember a forty-nine-year-old woman who began her career as a freshman at a large university, working in the development office. Thirty years later she resigned as a vice president to form her own consulting company. She made this decision overnight.

"It happened rather quickly," she said, "when the senior executive came to me and told me of the next seven-year plan. Suddenly I thought of seven more years, and I felt I could not keep up my enthusiasm for my job. I just couldn't face it. The next day I made my move. I turned in my letter of resignation and surprised myself with how fast I moved.

"I had no real plan, no job lined up, but ever since I was a little girl I had always known that I would someday have my own company. It just took me a long time to get there.

It was almost as though this idea was written into my life. It was something I expected to happen when the time was ripe, though the time was not ripe when I did it."

She created a company that was an extension of the work and skills she had mastered over three decades. She borrowed $10,000 to buy a computer, pay the first month's rent on an office, and rent a car. She opened her business in January and had paid back the debt by April. When she made her move, she was already there mentally. The financial part was a surprise; she had given herself a year.

The first thing she had to live through was the act of making the change, dealing with the fear of the unknown. Once she acknowledged that she was on her feet and exhilarated over the accomplishment, she felt great. She also knew that this was not the last venture she would try. She told me, "I have been in the process of bringing together all of the disparate elements about myself that most excite me."

If she had come to me for advice, which she didn't, I would have said, "Don't be afraid to be afraid. Use the fear as a guide would use a flashlight in a pitch-black cave. Move slowly, wisely, and stay alert."

I did ask her what she would advise others to do. "I wasn't typical. I didn't have a plan. I just jumped. Some of my advice would be if you don't have a lot of self-confidence, then make sure you have most of your pegs in the right holes before you change. If you are a positive thinker, it will work out some way. If you have a lot of questions don't let the fact that you can't answer all of them keep you from making a change. I know people who turn legitimate questions into obstacles and then stop. If you can't answer all of the questions but you have enough self-confidence, then do it and do it with passion."

When I began this chapter I asked you to pack a suitcase to take into the future. I suggest you travel light and leave enough space for a future. Of course, in my suitcase, I'm also packing some questions:

- Do I have an outlet for creative expression?
- Do I make things with my hands?
- Are my connections to family and friends deep and broad enough to sustain me to the end of my life?
- Do I nurture younger friends so that I remain connected?
- How do I get enough affection?
- How do I express my sensuality?
- Where do I derive status?
- What is the basis of my finances, and how long will they last?
- How do I take care of myself with regard to diet and exercise?
- What surroundings can I flourish in?

- How do I use my mind?
- What do I need to do to create balance in my life?
- Can I laugh at myself and at life?

Science may one day extend life through genetic engineering, but you'll still be confronted with the dilemma of what to live for and how to live a life with meaning.

And so, in a way, you are an artist who owns but one canvas. Either you can make the same painting layer upon layer with variations on the same theme or you can continue to enliven that canvas all the days of your life by experimenting with color, brush strokes, and new techniques and maybe even create something original, something uniquely you.

CHAPTER 9

Writing Your
Autobiography ≤

THE stories we tell about our lives are glimpses into our histories. In a lifetime we may tell the same story dozens of times, and when we're no longer around to tell the story, someone else will and so it goes. Nobel Prize winner Elie Wiesel spoke about the importance of keeping memories alive. Without memory, he said, you are a book without pages.

In the second fifty, once you realize after looking back that your life for the most part created you, you are ready now to create a life. Take with you the valuable lessons you learned from your own experiences and leave behind the misery you had to endure for living them. Ideally, writing and sharing your autobiography will help you see the unity and purpose in your life. But autobiography is also a process where you can begin a new chapter of your life any time you want. You have time in your second fifty to give new meaning to your life.

The actual writing is stimulated by thousands of associations, often by photographs or objects in the room in which you've chosen to write. A journalist friend who had trouble writing in the first person began by describing where he was in the present—the color of the sofa he was sitting on, the pictures, the view from his window, the weather outside, anything that helped him with time and place in that moment. Once he had set the scene in the present, he leaped back into his past.

One man decided that he wanted to write about only the last ten years. He was a gifted man who since birth had been regarded as a golden boy. He was talented, good-looking, and academically brilliant. He went to an Ivy League university and a top business school, then married and had children. Everything came easily to him and he believed in his own omnipotence, which was both a blessing and a curse—a blessing because he had self-confidence and kept testing his limits, and a curse when he overextended himself and went millions of dollars into debt.

It took him ten years to recover, and he is still paying back his creditors, but he reconstituted his original business because he wanted to get it right the second time. "It is my personal redemption," he said. He consciously monitors himself by using his past mistakes as examples of what not to do. He is his own teacher. He altered his life by studying his own lessons. Now, as he approaches sixty, he says he's fifty with ten years deducted for foolish behavior.

Over the years, I've been directly involved with over three hundred people writing their autobiographies. I've watched strangers become friends and whole groups turn into late-in-life families. I continue to be amazed at how resilient people are. Most don't even know how impressive they are until they tell their stories to others. "By God, I matter!" one woman exclaimed.

People reveal a remarkable capacity to adapt to the many challenging conditions of life. Many people begin their autobiographies at a time of turmoil—the loss of a job, a marriage, or a loved one; children moving away—and are uplifted when they reflect on how they have been able to overcome adversity. We tend to forget how good we are.

One woman couldn't believe how she was able to raise two preschoolers, work part-time, and go to graduate school at night. "I'm always cutting stories out of the newspapers about heroes. I reviewed my life and found a hero in myself," she said.

We also tend to forget how connected we feel to ordinary people who triumph over adversity. I have seen people with the most diverse of backgrounds find commonality in the emotions aroused by someone else's experience. An elderly black woman, for example, told a story to a group

in southern California about when she was a girl walking
to school down a dirt road in Mississippi. A bus full of
white children drove past her, leaving a layer of dust on
her clean white dress. She remembered the smiling faces
looking at her through the back window. They were on
their way to a newly constructed school while she was
headed to an old wooden building a mile away. She vividly
described the sensation of tears as they ran down her
cheeks, leaving tracks on her dusty face.

The group listened intently as she described the most
important branching point of her life: the moment when
she decided to become an educated woman. "I overcame
poverty," she said. "I could not overcome the pain of rac-
ism, but I don't suffer anymore." The group was silent
after she finished her story until one woman said, "What a
triumph you are!"

The next triumph is yours. The end of this book is the
beginning of your story.

Getting Started

Starting your autobiography is a bit like walking into an
attic where things have been stored for many years. Piles
of memories are waiting to be brought out into the light,
appreciated once again, organized, and shared with others.

Memories have to be organized around some main

themes in life. These themes have been useful to people doing their autobiographies. They bring significant life experiences to the surface.

Along with the themes, sensitizing questions are designed to encourage the flow of memories and to help you retrieve lost details about how you experienced growing up and maturing. Sensitizing questions are not supposed to be answered literally. They get you thinking about your life and encourage the flow of ideas. Some will cast a light on early forgotten pieces of your past. If a question does not prompt the recall of old memories, skip it and go on to the next one.

THEME ASSIGNMENT 1:

THE MAJOR BRANCHING POINTS IN YOUR LIFE

Think of your life as a branching tree, as a flowing river that has many juncture points, or as a trailing plant that puts down roots at various places and then grows on. Branching points are events, experiences, or happenings in our lives that significantly affect the direction or flow of our life.

Sensitizing Questions

1. About how old were you at the time of your first branching point? The timing of an event is often very important. Did yours happen too soon? Were you too young? Did it happen too late? Were you too old?

(*155*)

2. Who were the significant people involved in your turning point? Father, mother, spouse? You alone? Often
   you'll notice that the same people are involved again
   and again in major life turning points.

3. What emotions did you experience at the time the
   branching point occurred? How intense were these feelings? Do not be concerned if your feelings seem contra-
   dictory.

4. Sometimes our feelings about an experience or event
   change over time. Something that seemed like a disaster
   when it happened may turn out to be a positive event
   later on and vice versa. What emotions do you experience as you think about the turning point now?

5. How much personal choice was involved in this
   branching point? How much personal control did you
   have? Who or what was the external influence?

6. Branching points change our lives in one way or in
   many important ways. In your view, what are the ways
   your life was changed because of this first branching
   point? What effect, impact, or consequences did it have
   on your life? How would your life have been different if
   it had not occurred?

THEME ASSIGNMENT 2:
YOUR FAMILY

The history of your family includes your family of origin (grandparents, parents, siblings, uncles, and aunts) as well as your family of adulthood (spouse, children, grandchildren). You should mention only the family members who were important in shaping your life, not necessarily all the family members. Which family members played a major part in shaping your life? Why? What would another person have to know about your family in order to understand you and how you've come to be the person you are?

Sensitizing Questions

1. Who held the power in your family? How did you know?
2. Who offered support, warmth, and nurturing? Whom did you go to for comfort? Whom did you confide in?
3. What family member have you been closest to?
4. What family member did you know the least?
5. Did you like your family?
6. What did you like best about your family? Least?
7. Were you afraid of anyone in your family?
8. Who were the heroes in your family? Who were the family favorites? How did you know?
9. What were the major areas of conflict in your family?
10. What were the stated and unstated rules in your family?

11. Were you loved? How did you know? Did you feel loved?

THEME ASSIGNMENT 3:
YOUR WORK OR CAREER

Usually we think of work as something outside the home that requires imagination and energy to accomplish. A life's work can also mean being a husband, wife, or parent or a devoted religious person or someone dedicated to the arts. It may or may not involve a salary. One person can have a number of careers. What has been your major life's work or career?

Sensitizing Questions

1. How did you get into your major life's work? How was the decision made? What were the influences that contributed to your decision?
2. When did you formulate your early career goals? What did you want to be when you grew up? What and who were your influences? How much choice did you have?
3. What have been the ups and downs of your career? What were the setbacks, advances, and changes?
4. Have you had a series of similar careers or different ones?
5. If you have no major life's work, what would you like to do?

6. If you feel you have finished your life's work, how do you evaluate it?

7. Has your work provided new options?

8. Are you on schedule in your career, or are you ahead of or behind your own expectations?

9. What challenges, successes, problems, and failures have you experienced?

10. What have you enjoyed most about your work experiences?

11. What have you disliked about the jobs you've had?

THEME ASSIGNMENT 4:
THE ROLE OF MONEY IN YOUR LIFE

Money is one of the most important themes in life. It has both an obvious influence and a subtle influence. Attitudes about money are shaped by positive and negative influences.

Sensitizing Questions

1. What were you taught about money? Was money scarce or plentiful when you were growing up?

2. How important is it for you to make money?

3. Does money have any relationship to love in your life? How?

4. What was the first time you earned money? How did you feel about it? How did it affect your later ideas about money?

5. What have been your greatest financial successes?

6. What have been your worst financial failures?

7. Is money related to your self-esteem? How?

8. How often do you think about money? Do you worry about money?

9. Do you regard yourself as generous or stingy?

10. Have you ever borrowed money? How did you feel about it? Did you pay it back?

11. Are you a good or poor manager of money?

12. Do you ever give money away? How did that make you feel?

THEME ASSIGNMENT 5:
HEALTH AND BODY

Your image of your body and your health involves comparison with other persons and whether you feel strong or weak, coordinated or clumsy, attractive or unattractive.

Sensitizing Questions

1. What was your health like when you were a baby? Child? Adolescent? Young adult? Middle-aged adult? Older adult?

2. Were you considered a sickly child? How did that affect your self-image?

3. Were you ahead or behind in physical growth as a child and adolescent?

4. What health problems have you experienced in your life? How did you handle these problems?

5. How does your body react to games and sports?

6. How does your body react to stress? What do you do in response to your body's stress signals?

7. What have you done during your life to help or hurt your health?

8. How would you describe your physical appearance as a baby? Child? Adolescent? Young adult? Middle-aged adult? Older adult?

9. What parts of your body do you like most? Least? How has that changed over your life?

10. What have you done to change or improve your health and physical appearance during your life?

THEME ASSIGNMENT 6:
YOUR SEXUAL IDENTITY, SEX ROLES, AND SEXUAL EX-
PERIENCES

What has been the history of your development, including the development of your identity as male or female, your concepts of appropriate sex-role behavior, your sexual experience?

Sensitizing Questions

1. When did you first realize that you were a boy or a girl? How did you feel?

2. What toys did you use and what games did you play when you were a child? Were any toys or games forbidden?

3. How were you dressed as a child? What significance did your clothes have on your sexual identity?

4. Were you a tomboy? A sissy? A fraidycat? Did you ever wish you were the opposite sex?

5. What were the rules for being a boy or a girl?

6. Where did you get your sex education?

7. What were your early sexual experiences? Did you have childhood sweethearts?

8. Have you had any traumatic sexual experiences?

9. What have been your concepts of the ideal man or woman? How have your ideas changed?

10. What is your concept of the ideal relationship between two people?

11. How do you relate to members of the opposite sex? How do you relate to members of your own sex?

12. How would you characterize the history of your sexual experiences? What circumstances have affected your sexual identity and sexual experiences?

13. Have your ideas about sexual behavior changed over time?

14. What was the best sexual experience you ever had?

THEME ASSIGNMENT 7:

DEATH

How have your experiences with death affected your life and your character? How have your reactions to death changed over the years?

Sensitizing Questions

1. What was your first experience with death and how did it affect you?
2. How was death talked about and treated in your family? Did it frighten you? In what way did you understand it?
3. When did you go to your first funeral? How did you react?
4. Did you ever think you might die?
5. How do you grieve?
6. Do dead family members continue to have an effect on your life?
7. Do you feel guilty about anyone's death? Helpless? Angry? Resentful? Abandoned? Have you ever felt responsible for anyone's death?
8. Has the death of a famous person ever affected you?
9. What kind of a death would you like to have?
10. If you could talk to a dead person, who would it be? What would you ask or say?

11. What was the most significant death you have experienced? How did it change your life?
12. What have you taught your children about death?

THEME ASSIGNMENT 8:
LOVE AND HATE

The emotions of love and hate create, in their own way, an attachment to another person. They exist in the absence of logic and test the human capacity for compassion, evil, selflessness, and sadism.

Sensitizing Questions
1. What persons, places, or things aroused your greatest feelings of love when you were a child?
2. Who was your first love?
3. Who in your life made you feel loved and why?
4. Were you ever consumed by love? When and under what circumstances?
5. What role has love played in your life? How has that role changed over time?
6. How did your loves end?
7. What places, people, events, characteristics of people, objects, ideas, or kinds of behavior cause you to feel extreme dislike?
8. Have you ever hated someone so much you wished he or she would die?

9. How did you express your hatred?
10. How do you express your love?
11. How do people accept your love?
12. How do you accept love?
13. Do you have some strong unexpressed feelings of love for someone? Who is it and what prevents you from expressing your feelings?

THEME ASSIGNMENT 9:
EXPERIENCES WITH STRESS

A stress reaction can save your life or make it hell. It can be short-lived or it can paralyze. Life itself can be one big stressful journey, and then there are the lesser stresses of missing an airplane, losing your homework, humiliating yourself in front of thousands, and going broke. Whatever its cause, stress requires some adaptation and problem-solving.

Sensitizing Questions
1. How have you known you were stressed? What body signs or symptoms did you develop?
2. What have been the continuing or chronic stresses in your life? What were the short-lived stresses?
3. Do you cope with stress or try to correct the cause? How do you cope? What procedure do you use in attempting to solve the problem?

4. Who were your models for coping with stress?

5. What are your self-induced stresses? What stresses do you have no control over?

6. Under what circumstances do you collapse and become unable to cope with stress? How has this changed over the years?

7. Are you self-critical? How long do you think about a mistake?

8. Do you create stress for other people? In what circumstances?

9. How did you upset people when you were a child? What was their reaction? Were you punished? How?

10. Which actions were punished the most severely?

THEME ASSIGNMENT 10:
YOUR LIFE MODELS

A model is someone you want to pattern yourself after. It can be someone you admired from a distance—a hero that you have read about or seen on television. Models can also be family members or peers. Sometimes we find our models in books, or we create a fantasy model. Our values sometimes come from the models we've adopted.

When we are young we often have a single personal model. Later we trade in or trade up our models and shift within the family. Later still we create a composite model with traits from various people. In later life we may forget the origin of our models and live according to an internal standard of what we want to be like.

Sensitizing Questions

1. Who was your first model?
2. Which of your model's characteristics did you emulate?
3. When you went to school, who was your model of how to behave?
4. Describe the teachers who made an impression on you. What was it about them that you incorporated?
5. When did you break away from your early models and begin to create new ones?
6. Can you trace the way you express anger to someone from your childhood?
7. Who were the models for the ways you think of mealtime?
8. Did you have models for the way you react to rules?
9. Did you have models for expressing anger or violence?
10. As a mature adult can you identify the traits in your composite model person and trace where they came from?
11. Has another adult or a child ever used you as a model? What about you did that person model?
12. How did you react to being a model?

Here are more themes that may spark some memories:

1. The role of music, art, and literature in your life
2. The role of food
3. The role of leisure and recreation
4. The role of spirituality and religion
5. The role of power and politics
6. The role of school and education
7. The history of your fears
8. The history of your anger, rage, and depression
9. The history of drugs and alcohol
10. The history of accidents
11. The role of holidays and vacations

EPILOGUE ✑

I AM grateful to the people who generously shared their lives with me and contributed to my thinking about how our values evolve as we grow up. Over the years some of my thoughts have been published, but I have continued to rewrite the list. I was interested in ideas that I could use to guide my life and that also had some practical impact on the world we all share. Maybe you have some of your own to add.

I will not write my final chapter, but I do have some ideas about how I want to be remembered.

I deliberately began with a statement about children. Adults understand that the well-being of children is profoundly connected to the advancement of a civilized society. But there's something more personal at stake: I believe how we honor children is a test of how loving we are as individuals and as a nation.

About Being an Adult

To honor my children and all children, to foster their growth, and to remain close to them.

To keep a joyous spirit and avoid becoming bitter if I am overlooked by the young or by the events of the times.

To continue to learn so that I may be a resource for solving or moderating the problems of life.

To continue to weed the garden of my life, remove yesterday's flowers and dead branches, so that I may foster personal growth in myself.

To refrain from seeking an unreasonable share of resources and placing a disproportionate load upon others if I become ill.

Epilogue

To jettison old resentments and prejudices, so that I may
be emotionally free and intellectually open to others.

To use the experiences of my years to obtain fairness and
justice for others, so that I may remain an active citizen
in a free society.

To manage the passing on of possessions with fairness and
avoid manipulating them to gain attention or to cause
loved ones to vie for material gain.

To prepare myself and others for my death, so I may pass
with poise, dignity, and peace. (And to consider donat-
ing my body parts to others.)

To leave the land and its people better than I found them
by my own deeds and through the efforts of others
whom I have influenced.

James E. Birren, Ph.D., is associate director of the UCLA Center on Aging and Adjunct Professor of Medicine/Gerontology at UCLA. He lives in Pacific Palisades, California.

Linda Feldman is an award-winning journalist whose column on aging appeared in the *Los Angeles Times*. She has also written for *Rolling Stone* and *McCall's*. She lives in Santa Cruz, California.